MONEY ISN'T EVERYTHING

1001 WAYS

Low-Cost Ideas   *Proven Strategies*

TO REWARD

Achievement Awards ★ *Contests*

EMPLOYEES

...me off ★ *Case Studies* ★ *Praise*

BY BOB NELSON

Foreword by Ken Blanchard, coauthor of *The One Minute Manager*

UPC

0 19628 03339 0

"The most interesting and inventive business book on the market today . . . a publishing phenomenon." —*TRAINING* MAGAZINE

"Better than money: Praise and personal gestures motivate workers. Things that don't cost money are ironically the most effective."
—*THE WALL STREET JOURNAL*

"Welcome to Bob's World: A place of above-average managers and workers, all committed to personal excellence, good will and, of course, company profits. [This book] details how a little praise goes a long way." —*THE PHILADELPHIA INQUIRER*

"There's a difference between having someone show up for work and bringing out the best thinking and initiative in each person. To do that requires treating employees more as partners, not as subordinates. Being nice isn't just the right thing to do, it's also the economical thing to do." —*SEATTLE POST-INTELLIGENCER*

"[Helps managers] take certain rewards and mold them into new management styles at their companies." —*THE NEW YORK TIMES*

"Crammed with tips on how to motivate all types of workers, through both formal and informal incentive and recognition programs. If you don't have a budget for recognition, here are lots of low-cost incentives." —*INCENTIVE* MAGAZINE

"This blockbuster guide does wonders for morale! . . . use of its ideas is changing the face of rewards and recognition in the workplace."
—*SUCCESS* MAGAZINE

"A must read for anyone in business." —*SMALL BUSINESS FORUM*

BOOKS BY BOB NELSON

1001 Ways to Energize Employees
1001 Ways to Take Initiative at Work
365 Ways to Manage Better Page-A-Day® Perpetual
Motivating Today's Employees
Managing for Dummies
Consulting for Dummies
Empowering Employees Through Delegation
Delegation: The Power of Letting Go
Decision Point: A Business Game Book
Exploring the World of Business
The Perfect Letter
We Have to Start Meeting Like This: A Guide to Successful Meetings
Better Business Meetings
The Presentation Primer: Getting Your Point Across
Making More Effective Presentations
Louder and Funnier: A Practical Guide to Overcoming Stage Fright
The Supervisor's Guide to Controlling Absenteeism
The Job Hunt: The Biggest Job You'll Ever Have

1001 WAYS
TO REWARD
EMPLOYEES

BY BOB NELSON

WORKMAN PUBLISHING
NEW YORK

Library of Congress Cataloging-in-Publication Data
Nelson, Bob, 1956-
1001 ways to reward employees / by Bob Nelson.
p. cm.
Includes bibliographical references and index.
ISBN 1-56305-339-X
1. Incentives in industry.   I. Title.
HF5549.5.I5N45 1994
658.3'14—dc20   93-1449
CIP

Cover design by Lisa Hollander.
Cover and interior illustrations by Stephen Schudlich.

Workman books are available at special discounts when purchased in bulk for premiums and sales promotions as well as for fund-raising or educational use. Special editions or book excerpts can also be created to specification. For details, contact the Special Sales Director at the address below.

Workman Publishing Company, Inc.
708 Broadway
New York, NY 10003

First printing January 1994
Manufactured in the United States
40 39

Many thanks to the following people for granting permission to use excerpts from their work:

Numerous excerpts and quotes from *Incentive,* 355 Park Avenue South, New York, NY 10010. Copyright © 1988, 1989, 1990, 1991, 1992, 1993. Reprinted by permission of *Incentive.*

Excerpts from "Offbeat Options for Any Budget" by Melissa Capanelli. Copyright © April 1992. Reprinted by permission of *Sales & Marketing Management.*

Excerpts from *Recognition Redefined: Building Self-Esteem at Work* by Roger L. Hale and Rita F. Maehling, Tennant Company, P.O. Box 1452, Minneapolis, MN 55440-1452. Copyright © 1992. Reprinted by permission of the author.

Excerpts from "Holiday Gifts: Celebrating Employee Achievements" by Rosabeth Moss Kanter. Copyright © 1986 by Rosabeth Moss Kanter, Class of 1960 Professor at Harvard Business School and Chairman of Goodmeasure, Inc., Cambridge, MA. Reprinted by permission of the author.

Sidebars from "What Leaders Really Do" by John P. Kotter, May/June 1990. Copyright © 1990 by the President and Fellows of Harvard College; all rights reserved. Reprinted by permission of *Harvard Business Review.*

Numerous excerpts from *The 100 Best Companies to Work for in America* by Robert Levering, Milton Moskowitz and Michael Katz. Copyright © 1985 by Robert Levering, Milton Moskowitz and Michael Katz. Reprinted by permission of Addison-Wesley Publishing Company.

Statistics and quotes from "What Motivates Best?" by Christina Lovio-George. Copyright © April 1992. Reprinted by permission of *Sales & Marketing Management.*

Several quotes on rewards and recognition by Catherine Meek, President, Meek and Associates, 1055 Wilshire Blvd. Suite 1503, Los Angeles, CA 90017. Copyright © 1993. Reprinted by permission of the author.

ACKNOWLEDGMENTS

The following individuals were instrumental in making this book a reality:

Dr. Joe Maciariello of The Peter F. Drucker Graduate Management Center of The Claremont Graduate School for giving me the initial inspiration for this book and for his work in the area of reward systems.

At Blanchard Training and Development, Inc.: Dr. Ken Blanchard for his encouragement and support of this book and for serving as a mentor, manager, friend and living example of these principles in action; Michele Jansen for her creative input, research and enthusiasm for this book; and Krista Harrison for her assistance with research and administrative support. Extensive research assistance was also provided by Charlene Ables and Steve Berry.

At Workman Publishing: Peter Workman and Sally Kovalchick for their vision and support for this book; Eddy Herch, Carbery O'Brien, David Schiller, Barbara Perris and Mary Wilkinson for helping with the myriad of details in shaping the content and format of the manuscript; and Andrea Glickson and Janice Pomerance for their initial promotional efforts.

At McBride Literary Agency: Margret McBride, Winifred Golden and Susan Travis for their ongoing encouragement, suggestions and support.

And Jennifer Nelson for her ongoing help, support and never-ending patience.

FOREWORD

If there's one thing I've learned in my life, it's the fact that *everyone* wants to be appreciated. This goes for managers as well as employees, parents as well as children, and coaches as well as players. We never outgrow this need and even if it looks like we are independent and self-sufficient, the fact is we need others to help us feel valued.

Although this might sound like common sense, so often I've found that common sense is not common practice in organizations today. We're often too busy or too stressed to remember that the recognition we crave, others crave as well. For that reason, this book is a godsend to every well-intentioned manager or frustrated employee. It makes a compelling case that recognition, rewards and positive reinforcement all do work and that they can work for you.

With *1001 Ways to Reward Employees,* praising, recognizing and rewarding employees just became a little easier. You can now provide the rewards and recognition that people in your life so richly deserve. Bob Nelson shows you when and how to use rewards to get the most from every employee. He highlights the research that demonstrates the success of these principles and offers a multitude of potent examples from companies across the country. He provides a treasure chest of ideas, inspiration and resources to enable you to make praising, recognition and rewards a permanent part of your management repertoire. This is one book that should be on every manager's desk!

No longer can managers deny the power and practicality of praising. No longer can they fail to recognize a deserving employee because they couldn't think of something to do to show their appreciation. No longer will employees passively accept being ignored or be content to get feedback once a year, if then, during a performance review. No longer will using praise, recognition and rewards be optional in managing people.

No employee seeks to be mediocre; all seek to be magnificent. With this book they can be. And in the process, any work environment can be productive, motivating and fulfilling.

Ken Blanchard, co-author of
The One Minute Manager

PREFACE

Few management concepts are as solidly founded as the idea that positive reinforcement—rewarding behavior you want repeated—works. In fact, in today's business climate, rewards and recognition have become more important than ever for several reasons:

• Managers have fewer ways to influence employees and shape their behavior. Coercion is no longer an option; managers increasingly must serve as coaches to indirectly influence rather than demand desired behavior.

• Employees are increasingly being asked to do more and to do it more autonomously. To support looser controls, managers need to create work environments that are both positive and reinforcing.

• Demographics predict that fewer workers will be available in the post-baby boom era and that those who do exist will likely have fewer skills than their predecessors. This new pool of employees have different values and expect work to be both purposeful and motivating.

• In tight financial times, rewards and recognition provide an effective *low-cost* way of encouraging higher levels of performance from employees.

Studies indicate that employees find personal recognition more motivational than money. Yet, it is a rare manager who systematically makes the effort simply to thank employees for a job well done, let alone to do something more innovative to recognize accomplishments.

In thinking about this paradox, I concluded that a primary reason why most managers do not more frequently reward and recognize employees is that they lack the time and creativity to come up with ways to do it. A book of ways to recognize employees would thus be a fun and useful resource.

To my pleasant surprise, research uncovered hundreds of unique strategies that managers have used and are using today. The project thus became a vehicle for giving this data a wider audience.

My hope is that you will use this book to experiment and learn the power of recognition and that, as a result, your workplace—and the employees in it—will become more positive, productive and enjoyable.

—Bob Nelson
San Diego, California

P.S. Many readers have reported to me that they use this book as a personalized motivation handbook by simply passing it around to their staff and having each person initial the ideas they like.

CONTENTS

APPENDIXES

INTRODUCTION

Results of a recent survey by the Council of Communication Management confirm what almost every employee already knows: that recognition for a job well done is the top motivator of employee performance.

Yet most managers do not understand or use the potential power of recognition and rewards. This is true even though 33 percent of managers themselves report that they would rather work in an organization where they could receive better recognition.

When a manager is apprised of the importance of this fundamental principle of human behavior, the typical reaction is to insist that employees would appreciate only rewards and forms of recognition that directly translate to their pocketbook—raises or promotions.

While money is important to employees, what tends to *motivate* them to perform—and to perform at higher levels—is the thoughtful, personal kind of recognition that signifies true appreciation for a job well done. Numerous studies have confirmed this. The motivation is all the stronger if the form of recognition creates a story the employee can tell to family, friends and associates for years to come.

* * *

This book deals with both informal and formal rewards and recognition. By "formal" I mean part of a predetermined program; "informal" here means more spontaneous. As for the distinction between rewards and recognition, Aubrey Daniels, a leading authority on performance management, explains it best: "You reinforce behaviors and reward results."

Part I of this book, "Informal Rewards," focuses on manager-initiated, performance-based rewards. The guidelines for effectively rewarding and recognizing employees are simple:

1. Match the reward to the person. Start with the individual's personal preferences; reward him or her in ways he or she truly finds rewarding. Such rewards may be personal or official, informal or formal, public or private, and may take the shape of gifts or activities. Janis Allen, performance management consultant and author of *I Saw What You Did and I Know Who You Are,* advocates having people who work for you complete a "reinforcer survey" of things they like, and suggests that you do one for yourself as well. Since preferred reinforcers differ from person to person, composing such lists is the best way to make sure your actions are as effective as they can be. Having employees initial items they like in this book is another way of determining what motivates them.

2. Match the reward to the achievement. Effective reinforcement should be customized to take into account the significance of the achievement. An employee who completes a two-year project should be rewarded in a more substantial way than one who simply does a favor for you. The reward should be a function of the amount of time you have to plan and execute it and the money you have to spend.

3. Be timely and specific. To be effective, rewards need to be given as soon as possible after the desired behavior or achievement. Rewards that come weeks or months later do little to motivate employees to repeat their actions. You should always say why the reward is being given—that is, provide a context for the achievement. Once you have consistently rewarded desired performance, your pattern of recognition may become more intermittent as the desired behavior becomes habitual with employees.

Part II, "Awards for Specific Achievements and Activities," presents specific awards organizations have used to obtain specific results in productivity, customer service, sales and so forth.

Part III, "Formal Rewards," reviews the company-initiated programs most commonly used to maintain motivation throughout the organization. The most effective rewards ultimately link to formal programs of some type. A thank-you letter or public praise can be a significant way of acknowledging a person's efforts and achievements, but if that is the only form of recognition a manager uses, such rewards will soon lose their effectiveness.

Here is a good rule of thumb: For every four informal rewards (e.g., a thank-you), there should be a more formal acknowledgment (e.g., a day off from work), and for every four of those, there should be a still more formal reward (e.g., a plaque or formal praise at a company meeting), leading ultimately to such rewards as raises, promotions and special assignments.

Catherine Meek, president of Meek and Associates, Los Angeles compensation consultants, offers guidelines to make reward and recognition programs effective:

☞ The programs should reflect the company's values and business strategy.

☞ Employees should participate in the development and execution of the programs.

☞ The programs can involve cash, noncash or both.

☞ Since what is meaningful to you may not be meaningful to someone else, the programs should encompass variety.

☞ The programs should be highly public.

☞ The programs have a short life span and must be changed frequently.

In addition, Aubrey Daniels recommends that leaders be held accountable for effectively recognizing employees and that organizations avoid using blanket or "silver bullet" approaches to motivation. "Jelly bean" motivation—giving the same reward to every member of the organization—not only does not inspire employees to excel, but it may actually damage performance as top achievers see no acknowledgment of the exceptional job they have done.

The Appendixes include lists of companies that can help you customize rewards and plan recognition activities.

1001 WAYS
TO REWARD
EMPLOYEES

PART I

INFORMAL REWARDS

This section suggests informal—that is, spontaneous—rewards and forms of recognition that can be implemented with minimal planning and effort by almost any manager.

In a recent study of more than 1,500 employees in scores of work settings by Dr. Gerald H. Graham, professor of management at Wichita State University, the most powerful motivator was personalized, instant recognition from their managers. "Managers have found," Graham adds, "that simply asking for employee involvement is motivational in itself."

In one of his studies, employees perceived that manager-initiated rewards for performance were made least often, and perceived that company-initiated rewards for presence (that is, rewards based simply on being in the organization) occurred most often. This was so even though the first type of reward has the highest motivational impact and the second type has lower impact. Graham's study determined the top five motivating techniques:

1. The manager personally congratulates employees who do a good job.

2. The manager writes personal notes about good performance.

3. The organization uses performance as the basis for promotion.

4. The manager publicly recognizes employees for good performance.

5. The manager holds morale-building meetings to celebrate successes.

Only 42 percent of the respondents believed that their managers typically used the top motivating technique in which a manager personally congratulates employees who do a good job. The other top factors were perceived by less than 25 percent of the respondents as being typically used.

Not only are informal rewards more effective, but they tend to be less expensive. According to the "People, Performance and Pay" study by the American Productivity Center in Houston and the American Compensation Association in 1987, it generally takes 5 to 8 percent of an employee's salary to change behavior if the reward is cash and approximately 4 percent of the employee's salary if the reward is non-cash.

The ideas in this section and in the rest of the book will be most effective if they are tailored to the individual preferences of the people being recognized. Thus, the way to begin is by asking your employees how you can best show appreciation when they have done a good job.

No-Cost Recognition

S ome of the most effective forms of recognition cost nothing at all. A sincere word of thanks from the right person at the right time can mean more to an employee than a raise, a formal award or a whole wall of certificates or plaques. Part of the power of such rewards comes from the knowledge that someone took the time to notice the achievement, seek out the employee responsible and personally deliver praise in a timely manner.

Research by Dr. Gerald Graham throughout the United States revealed that the type of reward employees most preferred was personalized, spur-of-the-moment recognition from their direct supervisors. In a recent survey of American workers, 63 percent of the respondents ranked "a pat on the back" as a meaningful incentive.

Since several studies on employees have shown that the greatest influence on job satisfaction is the supervisor, any manager has all the ingredients for achieving a high degree of satisfaction—and a correspondingly high level of performance—among his or her employees.

J oe Floren of Tektronix, Inc., a manufacturer of oscilloscopes and other electronic instruments located in Beaverton, OR, likes to tell the story of the You Done Good Award. A former communications manager, Floren recalls having coffee a number of years ago with his boss, a vice president. The boss said he'd been mulling over a problem stemming from the company's rapid growth. He thought the company was

☛ *Call an employee into your office just to thank him or her; don't discuss any other issue.*

☛ *Post a thank-you note on the employee's office door.*

☛ *Volunteer to do another person's least desirable work task for a day.*

☛ *Answer the person's telephone for a day.*

☛ *Have your company president or your manager's manager call an employee to thank him or her for a job well done, or have the same person visit the employee at his or her workplace.*

☛ *Wash the employee's car in the parking lot during lunch.*

getting so big that it needed a formal recognition program. He had read some personnel handbooks on the subject and began telling Floren about several variations on the gold watch traditionally given for time served.

The boss's proposition sounded ludicrous to Floren. The boss challenged Floren to come up with something better. Floren suggested drawing up a notecard called the You Done Good Award and letting any employee send it to any other employee.

To Floren's surprise, the vice president agreed. Floren had some notecards printed and started distributing them. They caught on, and the informal awards have become part of life in the company. "Even though people say nice things to you," Floren says, "it means something more when people take the time to write their name on a piece of paper and say it. Employees usually post them next to their desks."

———

P eggy Noonan, former President Reagan's speechwriter, tells in her book *What I Saw at the Revolution* about a personal note she received from the President. She had been writing for him for four months and had not yet met him. One day the President wrote "Very Good" on one of her speech drafts. First she stared at it. Then she took a pair of scissors and cut it off and taped it to her blouse, like a second-grader with a star. All day people noticed it and looked at her and she beamed back at them.

———

According to the department of Organization, Development and Training at Busch Gardens-Tampa, the company gives a Pat on the Back Award to employees who do an outstanding job, and sends a notice of the award to the employee's file.

———

John Plunkett, director of employment and training for Cobb Electric Membership Corporation in Marietta, GA, says, "People love to collect others' business cards. Simply carry a supply of your cards with you and as you 'catch people doing something right,' immediately write 'Thanks,' 'Good job,' 'Keep it up' and what they specifically did in two to three words. Put the person's name on the card and sign it."

———

All employees at Apple Computer in Cupertino, CA, who worked on the first Macintosh computer had their signatures placed on the inside of the product.

———

At Metro Motors in Montclair, CA, the name of the Employee of the Month goes up on the electronic billboard over the dealership. Similarly, the City of Philadelphia used an electronic message board that runs around all four sides of a downtown skyscraper to honor the head of the local school system: "Philadelphia congrats Dr. Constance Clayton on 10 years."

———

One-Minute Praising

✔ Tell people up front that you are going to let them know how they are doing.

✔ Praise people immediately.

✔ Tell people what they did right—be specific.

✔ Tell people how good you feel about what they did right and how it helps the organization and the other people who work there.

✔ Encourage them to do more of the same.

—KENNETH BLANCHARD and SPENCER JOHNSON, Adapted from *The One Minute Manager*

THE MOST BEAUTIFUL SOUND . . . YOUR NAME

☛ *A good way to personalize any reinforcer is to use the person's first name when delivering the comment. Tell him or her why the behavior or result is important to you.*

☛ *Greet employees by name when you pass their desks or pass them in the hall.*

☛ *When discussing an employee's or a group's ideas with other people, peers, or higher management, make sure you give credit.*

☛ *Acknowledge individual achievements by using employees' names when preparing status reports.*

☛ *Name a continuing recognition award after an outstanding employee.*

F ederal Express in Memphis inscribes the name of an employee's child in large letters on the nose of each new airplane it purchases. The company holds a lottery to select the name and flies the child's family to the manufacturing plant for the christening.

B ell Atlantic's cellular telephone division in Philadelphia names cell sites after top employees.

S am Colin, founder of Colin Service Systems janitorial services in White Plains, NY, used to go around handing out Life Savers candy to employees. That early tradition has developed into a lasting philosophy of recognition that today includes such awards as Most Helpful Employee and Nicest Employee. Coworkers vote for the employees they think should win the titles, and executives make the presentations.

X erox Corporation, headquartered in Stamford, CT, gives Bellringer Awards: When an employee is recognized, a bell is rung in the corridor. Pacific Gas & Electric rings a ship's bell every time someone has a noteworthy achievement.

BRAVO CARDS

Janis Allen, a performance management consultant, tells the story of a group of officers she was training in the Department of the Army. One person in particular, a colonel, showed great resistance to the use of any reinforcers. A week or so after the seminar, the colonel's manager—a general—wanted to praise him for his handling of an important presentation. The general found a piece of yellow construction paper, folded it in half and wrote "Bravo" on the front. Then he wrote his reinforcing remarks inside.

The colonel was called in, praised and handed the card. "He took it and read it," Allen says. "He didn't even look up when he finished. He just stood up abruptly without even making eye contact, turned and walked out of the office." The general thought, "Wow, I've done something wrong now." He thought maybe he had offended the colonel.

When the general went to check on the colonel, he found that he had stopped at every office on the way out and was showing off the "Bravo" card. He was smiling and everybody was congratulating him.

The colonel subsequently printed his own recognition cards with "Wonderful" on the front. They became his signature reinforcers.

---

66 In the twenty years I have been doing this and the thousands of employees I have interviewed in hundreds of companies, if I had to pick one thing that comes through to me loud and clear it is that organizations do a lousy job of recognizing people's contributions. That is the number one thing employees say to us. 'We don't even care about the money; if my boss would just say thank you, if he or she would just acknowledge that I exist. The only time I ever hear anything is when I screw up. I never hear when I do a good job.' Recognition programs are a very important element of your total compensation program. 99

—CATHERINE MEEK,
President,
Meek and Associates

At General Mills, headquartered in Minneapolis, new employees can pick a work of art for their office from a large collection. Similarly, those who work in individual offices choose their own furnishings and works of art at Mary Kay Cosmetics.

Low-Cost Rewards

A s you saw in the preceding section, many highly effective forms of recognition cost nothing. If you raise your available budget from nothing to a nominal amount (say less than $20), the number of potential reinforcers increases greatly. If you set your budget at $50, you can use a wide range of reinforcers. With a modest investment of time, energy and thoughtfulness, any manager can deliver a unique and truly memorable employee reward.

A Hewlett-Packard Company engineer burst into his manager's office in Palo Alto, CA, to announce he'd just found the solution to a problem the group had been struggling with for many weeks. His manager quickly groped around his desk for some item to acknowledge the accomplishment and ended up handing the employee a banana from his lunch with the words, "Well done. Congratulations!" The employee was initially puzzled, but over time the Golden Banana Award became one of the most prestigious honors bestowed on an inventive employee.

During Secretaries' Week at Mary Kay Cosmetics, all secretaries get flowers.

> 66 There are two things people want more than sex and money . . . recognition and praise. 99
>
> —MARY KAY ASH,
> Founder,
> Mary Kay Cosmetics

Tom Tate, program manager in the Personnel and Management Training Division of the federal government's Office of Personnel Management in Washington, DC, tells the story of the Wingspread Award. A beautiful engraved plaque was first given to the division's "special performer" by the department head. Later that person passed the award to another person who, he believed, truly deserved it. The award came to take on great value and prestige because it came from one's peers. A recipient can keep it as long as he or she wants, or until he or she discovers another "special performer." When the award is to be passed on, a ceremony and lunch are planned.

At Claire's Boutiques in Wooddale, IL, district managers reward a manager by working his or her store on a Saturday. The regional managers have a traveling trophy cup, which they fill with goodies (and items related to the award) as it is passed from one district manager to another.

Noreen Wahl, manager of human resources for Sherpa Corporation, a software company in San Jose, CA, emphasizes that it's not the award itself as much as the recognition. "We purchased an old bowling trophy that was ugly, gaudy and huge from a pawnshop to use as a "pass around" award for spectacular results achieved. Each recipient proudly displayed it while it was theirs."

Chris Giangrasso, director of management and organizational development for Philadelphia's ARA Services, which provides food and leisure services and textile rentals, suggests organizing a day of appreciation for a worthy person. ARA schedules a day in honor of the person (for example, Bob Jones Day), and the company sends a notice to all employees announcing the date and the reason for the honor. The honoree enjoys all sorts of frills, such as computer banners and a free lunch.

A CASE STUDY IN INFORMAL RECOGNITION

Elsie Tamayo explains how she improved the morale, pride and productivity of the training department when she was training director of the City of San Diego's Department of Social Services.

When Tamayo started, employee morale was low and the group's identity in the organization was weak. Tamayo met with the thirteen employees in her department and asked how they wanted to be perceived by the organization. The group created its own identity as the Training and Development Center, designed a logo and painted it on the exterior and in the lobby of their building. For the first time, everyone got business cards that showed the new logo.

Tamayo then announced that the group would spend one half day a month as a Reward and Recognition (R&R) Day, and that the group

CAPTURE THE MOMENT

☛ Create a Hall of Fame wall with photos of outstanding employees.

☛ Take a photo of the person being congratulated by his or her boss's boss. Frame the photo. Place photographs of top performers in the lobby.

☛ Make a photo collage about a successful project that shows the people who worked on it, its stages of development, and its completion and presentation.

☛ Create a "yearbook" to be displayed in the lobby that contains everybody's photograph, along with his or her best achievement of the year.

☛ Establish a place to display memos, posters, photos and so on, recognizing progress toward goals and thanking individual employees for their help.

☛ When paychecks go out, write a note on the envelope recognizing an employee's accomplishment.

☛ Ask five people in your department or company to go up to the person sometime during the day and say, "[Your name] asked me to thank you for [the task or achievement]. Good job!"

☛ Write five or more Post-it notes thanking the person for a job well done and hide them among the work on his or her desk.

would come up with things they wanted to do together. They took the train to Los Angeles to visit a museum, went shopping in Tijuana, and went to the zoo. They had no budget for these activities, so the employees paid expenses.

At each department meeting Tamayo solicited the help of one employee to come up with a fun way of rewarding another member of the group. To announce one employee's promotion, the group staged a parade through the building; another employee was presented with an Energizer bunny "because he kept going and going and going, helping others when needed"; someone who worked fast received a toy roadrunner. Tamayo started each department meeting by reading letters praising the department or people in it. At all times, she gave the group the latest information she had about developments in the organization.

Tamayo used numbers as recognition to increase the visibility of the group's achievements. The number of employees trained each month was tracked, as were cost-saving ideas, and progress was communicated throughout the organization. In the department, flip charts were hung tracking progress toward goals, and "master's degrees" were awarded to trainers and managers who trained 1,000 hours.

Tamayo bartered her services with other training companies to get slots for her group members or facilities for an off-site retreat. She also started a self-development library and made use of it a reward.

She used extensive spontaneous rewards,

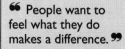
such as a quick handwritten note or a note on a flip chart that read, "You really handled the meeting well yesterday," including specific remarks on why the activity was important, and posting the flip chart on the person's door. She often let group members come in late the day after finishing a training session.

Once a week, every person met with Tamayo for an hour to talk about anything. Initially many of the meetings lasted less than ten minutes, but over time everyone came to use the full hour. An employee might discuss the results of a training session and how he or she could improve, problems with other employees, or ways to improve skills and career potential.

Tamayo hosted a make-believe marathon for all project members. T-shirts and "records" — old LPs with specially made up jackets were handed out to recognize individuals' achievements during a mock marathon celebration.

All these activities cost little or no money, and throughout employees knew they still had to put in the hours needed to get their jobs done. Within several months the morale, excitement, pride and energy of the department skyrocketed, and the group was held in higher esteem by the rest of the organization.

———

At Busch Gardens-Tampa, employees who offer exceptional service to guests receive a "scratch-off" card. These cards are issued on the spot by the management staff and can be redeemed for a variety of rewards.

———

> **" People want to feel what they do makes a difference. "**
>
> —FRANCES HESSELBEIN,
> President,
> The Drucker Foundation

☛ Conduct an Out-to-Dinner program for employees. Award dinners for two for doing something special, like coming in on a day off or working through a break.

☛ Develop a Behind the Scenes Award specifically for those whose actions are not usually in the limelight.

☛ Name a space after an employee and put up a sign (The Suzy Jones Corridor, for example).

☛ Say thanks to your boss, your peers and your employees when they have performed a task well or have done something to help you.

LET'S DO LUNCH

☞ *Buy the person lunch as a form of thanks or to mark a special event. A secretary for an insurance company says her manager takes her to lunch every time he gets a promotion. "He does it because he feels I've helped him," she says. Another idea is to pay for a secretary to attend a local lunch or other events during Professional Secretaries' Week (some of these are meant to be attended by both secretary and manager).*

☞ *Authorize managers to walk around with lunch coupons so they can hand them out on the spot.*

☞ *Buy lunch for the person and three coworkers of his or her choice.*

☞ *Arrange for the employee to have lunch with the company president.*

☞ *Leave a card for a lunch date at the employee's discretion.*

☞ *Bring the person bagged lunches for a week.*

☞ *Have lunch or coffee with an employee or a group of employees you don't normally see.*

Robin Horder-Koop, manager of programs and services at Amway Corporation, the distributor of house and personal-care products and other goods in Ada, MI, uses these inexpensive ways to recognize the 200 people who work for her:

✔ On days when some workloads are light, the department's employees help out workers in other departments. After accumulating eight hours of such work, employees get a thank-you note from Horder-Koop. Additional time earns a luncheon with company officials in the executive dining room.

✔ All workers are recognized on a rotating basis. Each month, photos of different employees are displayed on a bulletin board along with comments from their coworkers about why they are good colleagues.

✔ Horder-Koop sends thank-you notes to employees' homes when they do outstanding work. When someone works a lot of overtime or travels extensively, she sends a note to the family thanking them for their support.

✔ At corporate meetings, employees play games such as Win, Lose or Draw and The Price Is Right, using questions about the company's products. Winners get prizes such as tote bags and T-shirts.

Other inexpensive ideas Horder-Koop uses include giving flowers to employees who are commended in customers' letters, having supervisors park employees' cars one day a month and designating days when workers can come in late or wear casual clothes to the office.

D r. Jo-Anne Pitera, director of corporate education and training for Florida Power and Light in North Palm Beach, suggests putting a flip chart by the elevator door where people can list thank-you's and successes for all to see. Pitera also recommends having department members submit nominations for outstanding efforts to be announced at staff meetings, perhaps in conjunction with a drawing for gifts or money.

☞ *Make a thank-you card by hand.*

☞ *Cover the person's desk with balloons.*

☞ *Find out the person's hobby and give an appropriate gift.*

☞ *Buy the person something to use in his or her hobby.*

☞ *Buy the person something for his or her child.*

MANAGER-INITIATED REWARDS AND RECOGNITION

T he following list was generated by sales managers at American President Lines transportation company in Oakland and submitted by Laird D. Matthews, director of sales training and development. Most of the rewards are designed to cost less than $100 and are completely controlled by local management, so they don't need corporate buyoff. Some are intended to provide a spark of humor.

✔ Letters from manager, managing director, vice president, president

✔ Personal phone calls from managing director, vice president, president

✔ Parking spot for Top Sales Rep of the Month

✔ Day off, half day off, Friday off

✔ Magazine subscription

FOOD FOR THOUGHT

☛ *Bake a batch of chocolate-chip cookies for the person.*

☛ *Make and deliver a fruit basket to the person.*

☛ *Tape a candy bar for the typist in the middle of a long report with a note: "Halfway there!"*

✔ Monthly rep certificate with name on plaque

✔ Meal with staff member, vice president or president

✔ E-mail acknowledgment

✔ Promotional gift, special memento

✔ Birthday card, cake, gift

✔ Award pin

✔ Team dinner, team outing

✔ Feature company personnel in training films

✔ Sales Rep of the Month/Quarter/Year Award

✔ Acting sales managership

✔ Conference attendance

✔ Tickets to events

✔ Bottle of wine or champagne

✔ Training/attendance award

✔ National accounts trip as "award-winning employee"

✔ Tour of West Coast

✔ Trip with account representative

✔ Weekend trips

✔ Open praise

✔ Letters of recognition

✔ Sales giveaway

✔ Recognition lunch

✔ Publication of recognition

✔ Leader of the Month (e.g., meetings)

✔ Plum assignment

✔ Increased territory

✔ Transfer of a nonproducing account

✔ One month of shoeshines

✔ Contribution to favorite charity

✔ Bulletin board notice

✔ Flowers, balloons or a bouquet

✔ One-month club membership

✔ Chance to represent company at an industry event (salesperson's choice)

✔ Dinner or a night on the town with spouse

✔ Training session at new location of choice

✔ Overseas training trip

✔ Sports jacket or suit

✔ Upgrade of CRT

✔ Sales meeting acknowledgment

✔ Lunch for everyone paid for by top performer

✔ Group day off event

✔ Massage, facial or manicure

✔ Round of golf

✔ Individual home computer

✔ Computer printer for home use

> 66 Recognition is so easy to do and so inexpensive to distribute that there is simply no excuse for not doing it. 99
>
> —ROSABETH MOSS KANTER,
> Author and
> Management Consultant

☛ Give an employee a copy of the latest best-selling management or business book or a subscription to a business journal.

☛ Inscribe a favorite book as a gift.

> **66** Compensation is what you give people for doing the job they were hired to do. Recognition, on the other hand, celebrates an effort beyond the call of duty. **99**
>
> —From "How to Profit from Merchandise Incentives," *Incentive*

✔ Dinner with managing director

✔ Hot-air-balloon ride

✔ Limousine ride

✔ Upgrading of company car

✔ Ship ride, harbor tour

✔ Company logo tattoo

✔ Gift certificate

✔ Tape deck for car

✔ Own office

✔ Better office location or arrangement

✔ Champagne brunch

✔ $50 cash

✔ Case of beer

✔ Toys for kids

✔ Presentation of honoree to visiting executives

✔ Invitation of staff to home

✔ Articles about staff in company newsletters

✔ Exposure to top management through task force or committee

✔ Relief from personal chores (e.g., wash car, cut lawn, etc.)

Recognition Activities

Many effective forms of recognition are one-time events that celebrate a significant achievement or a milestone. Such activities need to be planned so as to be timely and pertinent to the situation and the person being recognized.

A recent survey by the Minnesota Department of Natural Resources found that recognition activities contributed significantly to employees' job satisfaction. Most respondents said they highly valued day-to-day recognition from their supervisors, peers and team members. Other findings from the survey:

- 68 percent of the respondents said it was important to believe that their work was appreciated by others.

- 63 percent agreed that most people would like more recognition for their work.

- 67 percent agreed that most people need appreciation for their work.

- Only 8 percent thought that people should not look for praise for their work efforts.

Nancy Branton, project manager for the survey, says, "Recognition programs are more important now than in the past. Employees increasingly believe that their job satisfaction depends on acknowledgment of work performance as well as on adequate salary. This is especially true of employees who are highly interested in their work and take satisfaction in their achievements."

> 66 When manage-
> ment shows through
> actions rather than
> words that you're a
> valuable employee,
> that your input is val-
> ued no matter what
> level you work at, it's
> very motivating. 99
>
> —AARON MELICK,
> Circulation and
> Marketing Administrator,
> Playboy Enterprises

Hunter Simpson, the president of Physio-Control Corp., which manufactures medical electronics products in Redmond, WA, makes it a point to spend one hour with every new employee, at no matter what level.

Each new employee group at Viking Freight System in Santa Clara, CA, spends an hour with the president or another top officer during a one-day orientation. And everyone who joins Mary Kay Cosmetics meets with founder Mary Kay Ash during his or her first month.

A VIP Pass allows the recipient free privileges for a certain period (a month or a quarter) at Management 21 training and consulting firm in Nashville, according to Cheryle Jaggers, training coordinator. An honoree might receive free lunches in the cafeteria, free membership in the company's fitness center or free parking in the parking garage.

Joan Cawley, director of human resources at Advanta Corporation, a financial services company in Horsham, PA, uses the following forms of recognition: surprising internal service departments such as payroll and switchboard/reception with doughnuts or candy; treating female staff members to a lunchtime manicure during an especially hectic period; buying Teenage Mutant Ninja Turtle decorations for an employee too busy to plan a child's birthday party; presenting a monogrammed canvas briefcase to commemorate a staff member's promotion to management; surprising a department with a picnic at a local park, complete with champagne and strawberry shortcake made by the department head in place of a regular Friday staff meeting; and presenting a Life Saver Award—a dozen packs of Life Saver candies and a gift certificate from a local department store to recognize an employee's efforts in filling two jobs during a period of transition.

> 66 Men and women want to do a good job, a creative job, and if they are provided the proper environment, they will do so. 99
>
> —BILL HEWLETT, Cofounder, Hewlett-Packard

Catherine Meek of Meek and Associates, a compensation consultant firm in Los Angeles, reports about a hospital she worked with, "At any one time they had twelve to fifteen employee recognition programs going, each developed by employees. The janitors and housekeeping staff came up with the Golden Broom Award. They have these little cards made up with a golden broom on them, and if someone is seen picking up trash—other than a janitor—then he or she gets this award. After someone receives ten cards he or she gets something else—nothing really expensive or big, but it gets the message across.

"Another program is called the Guaranteed Service Program. It refunds a patient's money for nonsurgical procedures if the patient is not totally satisfied with the services. If a patient does not feel he or she was provided with the appropriate service, then the bill is refunded. This hospital has a fund for this, and every quarter what isn't returned to patients is raffled off to

> **"** The most important factor is individual recognition—more important than salaries, bonuses or promotions. Most people, whether they're engineers, business managers or machine operators, want to be creative. They want to identify with the success of their profession and their organization. They want to contribute to giving society more comfort, better health, more excitement. And their greatest reward is receiving acknowledgment that they did contribute to making something meaningful happen. **"**
>
> —PAUL M. COOK,
> Founder and CEO,
> Raychem Corporation

employees. What that does is focus employees on providing the best possible patient care, because the better the care, the higher the fund and the more money in their pockets.

"Another program is called Caught in the Act of Caring. If an employee, vendor or anyone catches you in the act of caring, you get a little card that says, 'I was caught in the act of caring.' After you get a certain number of these cards, you can trade them in for various merchandise, such as electronics equipment.

"None of this takes all that much time as long as you have employees involved in these various programs. The hospital doesn't really think of the time; it's just the way they do business."

———

At South Carolina Federal financial services in Columbia, the president and other top managers serve employees lunch or dinner as a reward for a job well done.

———

The Tennant Company, a manufacturer in Minneapolis, has a Positive Feedback Committee that each year sponsors a Positive Feedback Day, on which all employees receive "That-A-Way" notepads, pens printed with the phrase "Positive Strokes Only," balloons and signs. At holiday time, the committee sponsors an open house with cider and cookies and invites employees to drop by at scheduled breaks.

———

Empire of America Federal Savings Bank in Buffalo came up with Teller Recognition Week, during which tellers were showered with bouquets, boutonnieres and candy; certificates of appreciation; a breakfast in their honor; specially printed T-shirts; and a recognition party.

Patricia L. Keeley, training manager for Spectrum Emergency Care in St. Louis, recommends having an employee's dry cleaning picked up and delivered to the office for one month or having a catering service bring lunch to an employee every day for a week.

Ford Motor Company and AT&T use their employees in commercials.

Carla Levy, training specialist for Indianapolis Power and Light Company, recommends paying an employee's parking fees for a month or a year.

McDonald's has different motivational activities for its categories of workers, such as teenagers and older workers. "Thirty years ago, having an employee softball team was enough to satisfy workers," says Dan Gillen, staff director of store employment. "Today we have to tailor our incentives to the specific nature of our work force."

A district might hold a "senior prom," a chance for its older employees to meet and socialize outside work, or stage a potluck supper

---

The Ten Best Ways to Reward Good Work

Reward # 1:
Money

Reward # 2:
Recognition

Reward # 3:
Time off

Reward # 4:
A piece of the action

Reward # 5:
Favorite work

Reward # 6:
Advancement

Reward # 7:
Freedom

Reward # 8:
Personal growth

Reward # 9:
Fun

Reward # 10:
Prizes

—MICHAEL LEBOEUF,
The Greatest Management Principle in the World

☛ *Rent a sports car for the employee to drive for a week.*

☛ *Rent a billboard and put up a message featuring his or her picture and name.*

☛ *Create a "Good Tries" booklet to recognize those whose innovations didn't achieve their full potential. Be sure to include what was learned during the project so that this information can benefit others.*

☛ *Take the person to a midday movie.*

☛ *Give the employee a round of golf.*

in the restaurant or at a manager's home.

For its teenage workers, the company has established a flexible scheduling policy to accommodate student classes, exams and papers. "When I was captain of my soccer team and working during high school, I took off a month of work during the busiest part of the soccer season," Gillen says. On the day of the high school prom, workers might be brought in from other areas to cover for students who go to the prom.

———

Warren F. Doane, senior vice president of Founders Title Company in Redwood City, CA, suggests a wide variety of recognition rewards, including limousine rides to lunch and dinner, a stay at a bed-and-breakfast, a weekend at Lake Tahoe, a cruise on San Francisco Bay, a train ride to Reno, a baseball night for all employees, and an employees' lunch served by tux-clad managers.

———

Public Recognition/Social Rewards

Most employees perceive the use of personal and social reinforcers as highly desirable. Performance management consultant Janis Allen notes, "Surprisingly, many people say they
wish their organizations would give fewer tangibles and use more
social reinforcers. Most people are hungry for somebody to simply
look them in the eye and say, 'I like the way you do that.'"

Allen adds, "If people receive social reinforcement on the four-to-
one ratio (a minimum of four socials to one tangible) and receive reinforcers for behaviors, not only results, they will view the tangible as a
symbolic representation of appreciation. Then tangibles become items
which serve as reminders of the social reinforcement they have already
received. A tangible reinforcer carries the most impact when it symbol-
izes the recognized behavior or result."

In a recent survey, 76 percent of American
workers ranked recognition at a company
meeting as a meaningful incentive. At Blanchard
Training and Development in Escondido, CA,
employees exchange public praising at the end
of each company meeting.

> **❝** Many managers
> ignore or under-
> estimate the power
> of praise. **❞**
>
> —ROGER FLAX,
> President,
> Motivational Systems

> ❝ My main motiva-
> tion is the recogni-
> tion. It's very
> competitive and
> tough to move ahead
> here, so going to the
> awards luncheons
> and meeting the VPs
> is a good way of gain-
> ing visibility. My main
> purpose is to move
> ahead in my job, not
> to win a prize. If
> being a top per-
> former helps me get
> promoted, it's a
> means to an end. ❞
>
> —SARA NAVARRO
> Senior Sales
> Representative,
> United Services
> Automobile Association

☛ *Publicly announce
bonuses and raises.*

☛ *Invite employees to
your home for a special
celebration, and recog-
nize them in front of their
colleagues and spouses.*

Every four or five years, new store managers of J. C. Penney Corporation, headquartered in Dallas, are "affirmed" in a ceremony held at more than a dozen locations across the country. A pledge is made to the founding principles of the company, and at the conclusion each newly affirmed associate receives an HCSC pin, standing for Honor, Confidence, Service and Cooperation.

———

According to Robert Voyles, vice president for marketing services of Carlson Marketing Group in Minneapolis, "One way of ensuring that people are happier at work is to make sure they have friends at the company." That's one of the reasons behind the company's referral program for new hires. A worker receives a small reward when someone he or she referred is hired, then a larger one when the new person completes several months on the job. "When someone recommends someone else, he or she takes pride in—and feels responsible for—that person's work," Voyles says. "If the new person messes up, it's a reflection on the person who recommended him or her."

———

As part of Chicago-based Hyatt Hotel Corporation's "In Touch Day," all 375-plus headquarters employees—from the mail room to the executive suite—went to Hyatt properties around the country to provide guest services. Jim Evans, vice president of sales, spent several hours hailing taxis, loading luggage and collecting tips at the front door of the Hyatt Regency Chicago; Darryl Hartley-Leonard, president of Hyatt, served lunch in the employees' cafeteria, hailed cabs, checked in guests at the front desk and tended bar. "We're all working toward the same goal, but we corporate people forget what it's like," Hartley-Leonard said. "After a day like this, we know what on-line workers really go through."

> 66 We lead by being human. We do not lead by being corporate, professional or institutional. 99
>
> —PAUL HAWKEN,
> Founder,
> Smith & Hawken

One day a year at Mary Kay Cosmetics, all white-collar manufacturing employees work on the production lines.

One night during the Christmas holidays, The Walt Disney Company opens Disneyland to employees and their families only. Concessions and rides are run by upper managers who dress in costumes. Besides being a lot of fun, this event allows employees to see the theme park from the customer's perspective. A multitude of other programs builds a sense of camaraderie and identification with the Disney organization, including peer recognition programs and informal root-beer-float parties. Employee and customer satisfaction with Disney is among the highest in the industry and is the cornerstone of the company's success.

☛ *Offer a deserving employee a change in job title.*

☛ *Give the person a better office: larger, in a better location, better furnishings, etc.*

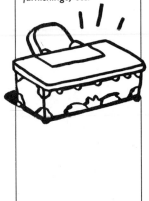

To demonstrate their trust in their employees, once a year all managers at Quad/Graphics printers in Pewaukee, WI, left the plant for twenty-four hours in the Spring Fling and Management Sneak. Normal printing operations continued while the managers held meetings and then went to the Milwaukee Art Museum. The company subsequently expanded the event into a two-day, three-evening affair, including managerial seminars at a local college. During the Fling, none of the managers is to set foot inside the printing plants unless an employee asks for emergency help. As of yet, no manager has ever been called in.

———

According to author and management consultant Rosabeth Moss Kanter, "Recognition—saying thank you in public and perhaps giving a tangible gift along with the words—has multiple functions beyond simple human courtesy. To the employee, recognition signifies that someone noticed and someone cares. What is the point of going all out to do something special if no one notices and it does not seem to make a whit of difference? To the rest of the organization, recognition creates role models—heroes—and communicates the standards: These are the kinds of things that constitute great performance around here." Following are some guidelines Kanter offers for successfully recognizing employees:

Principle 1: Emphasize success rather than failure. You tend to miss the positives if you are busily searching for the negatives.

Principle 2: Deliver recognition and reward in an open and publicized way. If not made public, recognition loses much of its impact and defeats much of the purpose for which it is provided.

Principle 3: Deliver recognition in a personal and honest manner. Avoid providing recognition that is too 'slick' or overproduced.

Principle 4: Tailor your recognition and reward to the unique needs of the people involved. Having many recognition and reward options will enable management to acknowledge accomplishment in ways appropriate to the particulars of a given situation, selecting from a larger menu of possibilities.

Principle 5: Timing is crucial. Recognize contribution throughout a project. Reward contribution close to the time an achievement is realized. Time delays weaken the impact of most rewards.

Principle 6: Strive for a clear, unambiguous and well-communicated connection between accomplishments and rewards. Be sure people understand why they receive awards and the criteria used to determine rewards.

Principle 7: Recognize recognition. That is, recognize people who recognize others for doing what is best for the company.

☛ Honor peers who have helped you by recognizing them at meetings. Mention the outstanding work or idea brought to your attention by an employee during your staff meetings or at meetings with your peers and management.

☛ Introduce peers and management to individuals and groups who have been making significant contributions as a way of acknowledging their work.

☛ Nominate employees for any of the company's formal award programs.

☛ Recognize (and thank) people who recognize others. Be sure it's clear that making everyone a hero is an important principle in your department.

Communication

Numerous motivational studies show that employees typically place a high value on getting information about their job, their performance and how the company is doing. When that communication is personal and timely, it is all the more highly valued.

In a recent study, positive written communication was found to be very important in motivating employees; however, this technique was used by only 24 percent of managers. A survey by Professional Secretaries International revealed that as many as 30 percent of professional secretaries would prefer a simple letter of appreciation from their managers—and that a bouquet or a lunch was unnecessary. Only 7 percent of respondents reported having ever received such a letter.

> **❝ The greatest motivational act one person can do for another is to listen. ❞**
>
> —ROY E. MOODY,
> President,
> Roy Moody and
> Associates

Performance management consultant Janis Allen advocates creating positive gossip—spreading positive comments about others. "When someone says something good about another person and I tell that person about it," Allen says, "she seems to get more reinforcement value from it than if she had received the compliment firsthand."

At American General Life in Nashville, a dozen employees are selected at random each month to meet the president and discuss matters of corporate concern.

Nissan Motor Manufacturing Corporation U.S.A., in Smyrna, TN, sponsors family orientation programs for new employees that include refreshments and a slide show about the company. Every family is given a set of drinking glasses with "Nissan" printed on them. The day before a new employee comes to work, several people call to welcome him or her to the company.

66 The leader needs to be in touch with the employees and to communicate with them on a daily basis. 99

—DONALD PETERSEN,
President and CEO,
Ford Motor Company

At Blanchard Training and Development in Escondido, CA, letters of praise from customers (and other employees) are reprinted in the company publication. First Chicago, a bank holding company, also does this, and gives each employee who receives such a letter two round-trip tickets, a Winning Spirit pin and a certificate signed by the president. First Chicago recognizes four to a dozen employees each month. At Collins & Aikman, a carpet manufacturer in Dalton, GA, the company recognizes and lists the achievements of employees' children in its newsletter.

☞ Plan to meet for informal chats with each of your employees at least once a week, finding out what aspects of their jobs they are focused on and how you can better assist them, and generally answering whatever questions they have about the department or company.

☞ When you hear a positive remark about an individual, repeat it to that person as soon as possible. Seek the person out if necessary. If you can't meet, leave an electronic mail or voice mail message.

Each morning at Precision Metalcraft in Winnipeg, Manitoba, management holds "huddles" to pass out the day's work assignments. The huddles end in a cheer as people disperse to get to work. To show they were all on the same team, Sheldon Bowles, chairman of the company, moved executives to the shop floor and used their offices to store the company's finished products.

A CASE STUDY IN CORPORATE COMMUNICATION

In his first two months as general manager of the new copy products group of Eastman Kodak in Rochester, NY, Chuck Trowbridge met with nearly every key person in his group, as well as with people elsewhere at Kodak who could be important to the copier business. Trowbridge set up dozens of vehicles to emphasize the new direction: weekly meetings with his own twelve direct reports; monthly "copy product forums" in which he met with groups consisting of a different employee from each of his departments; quarterly meetings with all 100 of his supervisors to discuss recent improvements and new projects; and quarterly State of the Department meetings, in which his managers met with everybody in their own departments.

Once a month, Bob Crandall, one of Trowbridge's direct reports and head of the engineering and manufacturing organization, and all those who reported to him also met with eighty to a hundred people from some area of Trowbridge's organization to discuss topics of their choice. Trowbridge and his managers met with the top management of their biggest supplier over lunch every Thursday. More recently, Trowbridge has created a format called "business meetings": His managers meet with twelve to twenty people to discuss a specific topic, such as inventory or master scheduling. The goal is to get all of his 1,500 employees into at least one of these focused business meetings each year.

☞ Use charts or posters to show how well an employee or group is performing.

Trowbridge and Crandall also enlisted written communication in their cause. A four- to eight-page "Copy Products Journal" was sent to employees once a month. A program called Dialogue Letters gave employees the opportunity to ask questions anonymously of Crandall and his top managers, with a guaranteed reply.

The most visible and powerful form of written communication was the charts. In a main hallway near the cafeteria, huge charts vividly reported the quality, cost and delivery results for each product, measured against difficult targets. A hundred smaller versions of these charts were scattered throughout the manufacturing area, reporting quality levels and costs for specific work groups.

Results of this intensive alignment process appeared within six months and remained evident more than a year later. These successes helped gain support for the new direction. In a four-year period, quality on one of the main product lines increased nearly 100 times. Defects per unit fell from 30 to 0.3. Over a three-year period, costs on another product line decreased nearly 24 percent. Deliveries on schedule increased from 82 percent to 95 percent in two years. Inventory levels dropped by more than 50 percent in four years, even though the volume of products increased. Productivity, measured in units per manufacturing employee, more than doubled in three years.

F ran Sims, executive director of Suncoast Management Institute, a management con-

> 66 Do all workers understand the mission of the company, the philosophy of senior management? To really feel included in the corporate culture, workers should know why the company exists, its basic values and the ways in which it cares for its customers. 99
>
> —RICHARD ROSS,
> President,
> Tri Companies

SAY IT IN WRITING

☞ *Write a "letter of praise" to employees to recognize their specific contributions and accomplishments; send a copy to your boss or higher managers and to the personnel department.*

☞ *Ask your boss to send a letter of acknowledgment or thanks to individuals or groups who make significant contributions. Have the CEO or a very senior manager write a letter of thanks.*

☞ *Send birthday cards to your employees' homes. Have the cards signed by the CEO.*

☞ *Write a congratulatory letter for special achievement that goes into the employee's file.*

sulting firm in St. Petersburg, FL, recommends writing a note to the employee's family at the end of a long project, thanking them for their support, acknowledging the good work their family member has done and explaining the importance of the project to the company.

Susan Eckel, director of Total Training Technology training consultants in Fairfax, VA, writes a formal recognition letter praising behavior she wants repeated and always sends a carbon copy to the employee's personnel file and to the president of the company. When employees receive an award in the company such as 19— Sales Rep of the Year or Rookie of the Year, she has that distinction printed under the person's name on new business cards. She also reports, "The use of a portable cellular phone for thirty days is very cherished. Make sure it's the smallest, catchiest one possible!" Every month the phone goes to someone new.

Security Pacific Corporation of Los Angeles has a Question Line with a toll-free number to respond to employees' job-related problems and queries.

Carillon Importers of Teaneck, NJ, the importers of Absolut vodka, and Air France recently started a joint program called Team Talk, designed to improve communication between employees and managers. Workers can call an 800 number to answer employee surveys and to leave comments and suggestions for managers. Callers gain "air points" redeemable for travel on Air France; some callers are "instant winners," capturing prizes such as personal stereos and phones.

———

Rosenbluth Travel in Philadelphia has an Associate of the Day program, in which any employee can spend a day with the company's CEO. Twice a year the company holds an employee focus group to discuss workplace issues. Every new employee spends two days at corporate headquarters, meeting top managers and performing in skits about good service experiences. The firm's officers also serve afternoon tea to new hires.

———

Lowell G. Rein, chairman of LGR Consultants in McMurray, PA, recommends several ways to reward employees by having them spend time with management:

✔ Have top managers visit the shop floor, talking informally with individual employees.

✔ Once a quarter, choose ten to twelve employees to dine with corporate executives.

✔ Have an outstanding employee spend a day with the CEO.

———

❝ Having some access to upper management is important in terms of how employees feel about the organization, and how they look at themselves. When employees know that the decision makers are accessible to them, they feel that their ideas are worth more. . . . Having everyone from the bottom up buying into what we're doing is worth something. ❞

—DARRELL MELL,
Vice President of
Telemarketing,
Covenant House

Companies Whose Top Management Regularly Meets With Employees

---

✔ Dana Corporation

✔ Electro Scientific

✔ Federal Express

✔ Johnson Wax

✔ Marion Labs

✔ Mary Kay Cosmetics

✔ Physio-Control

✔ Pitney Bowes

✔ Tandem Computers

✔ Viking Freight Systems

Executives of Tupperware, based in Kissimmee, FL, take thirty days on the road each year to spend time with their top 15,000 salespeople.

———

Home Depot, Inc., the home improvement supply stores headquartered in Atlanta, holds quarterly Sunday-morning meetings, affectionately dubbed "Breakfast with Bernie and Arthur" for the chairman and president of the company. All 23,000 employees are paid to come in and watch a forty-five minute program sent via satellite TV hookup. Bernard Marcus and Arthur Blank recap the company's performance over the past quarter, discuss growth plans and answer questions that employees phone in.

"Employees really like seeing the way Bernie and Arthur get along," says Tony Brown, a regional manager based near Atlanta. "They talk openly with each other, even when they disagree. But the best thing about these broadcasts is that workers see that Bernie and Arthur aren't afraid to share company details. In most companies there are sensitive topics that high officers want to sidestep, but not here. It makes people feel like they know exactly what's going on."

———

Once a year the president of H. B. Fuller Company, a maker of glues, adhesives and sealants in St. Paul, makes himself available to everyone in the company through what's called the President's Hot Line. Anybody can call him on that day at a special toll-free number to make suggestions for improving their products or to talk about anything else on their minds. The president usually gets between forty and fifty calls.

———

Every eighteen months the top managers of S.C. Johnson & Son (Johnson Wax), headquartered in Racine, WI, meet with all employees for a face-to-face question-and-answer session. At Inland Steel Industries in Chicago, spouses are invited to such informational meetings.

———

Twice a year, at Moog Automotive, a St. Louis maker of electrohydraulic control products, all employees are invited to attend a meeting with management at which they may ask any questions they want.

———

All Knight-Ridder publications have "management coffee breaks," during which each publisher meets with twenty to twenty-five rank-and-file employees for an hour and a half over coffee. Employees can send questions in advance. The year-end management meeting is held in a large hall so that all employees of the publications can attend.

———

Every three months, Physio-Control holds a meeting of all employees on company time. Employees are briefed on what's going on in the

> ❝ Nobody seemed to be in the dark. Everybody knew what was going on. There was none of the hush-hush atmosphere with management behind closed doors and everybody else waiting until they drop the boom on us. They are right down pitching in, not standing around with their hands on their hips. ❞
>
> —LONNIE BLITTLE, Assembly-line Worker, Nissan Motor Manufacturing Corporation U.S.A

Make Use of Newspapers to Praise Employees Publicly

✔ Send information about an accomplishment to the appropriate trade publication and the individual's hometown newspaper. Get your employees' pictures in the company newspaper.

✔ Write and publish a personal ad or publicity article in the local newspaper or company publication praising the person for a job well done.

✔ Take out a full-page advertisement in a local newspaper every year and thank every employee by name for his or her contribution.

company. Often much hoopla attends the meeting, such as a marching band hired for the occasion. Once a year at the end of the meeting, senior managers serve a pancake breakfast to the rest of the company.

———

H. J. Heinz, based in Pittsburgh, routinely shares information about employees at all levels of the organization in its internal publications and annual reports, including personal details about their lives, their off-the-job pursuits, and even their poetry.

———

Nick D'Agostino, owner of the D'Agostino's supermarket chain based in New Rochelle, NY, makes rounds of the company's twenty-four stores every week, chatting with workers and observing operations.

———

Tandem Computers in Cupertino, CA, has a tradition of Friday afternoon "beer busts" at which all employees can talk informally. If any employee wants to meet with the president, he or she can simply sign up in his appointment book.

———

At Hyatt Hotel Corporation "employees have the obligation, as well as the right, to communicate with managers," says Myrna Hellerman, vice president of human resources. The company holds monthly "Hyatt Talks," at which the general manager sits down with a randomly selected group of hotel staffers to talk informally about operations and procedures. Employees bring up issues and problems that are important to them, and within a week a member of the hotel's executive committee looks into the issue and responds in writing. "We want people to think of the hotel as 'my hotel,' a place they want to work," Hellerman says, "and these talks encourage the family feeling we try to have."

> 66 I'm open, honest and up front. As soon as I get information, employees get information. 99
>
> —NANCY SINGER,
> President,
> First of America Bank

M cDonald's encourages its franchisees to hold quarterly communication sessions. Usually the store owner sits down with a representative group of employees and listens to suggestions and gripes. "Things like realigning equipment or changing procedures—those get changed all the time due to workers' suggestions," says Dan Gillen, staff director of store employment. McDonald's supplies all its franchise owners with a manual outlining sample incentive programs they can adapt for their own establishments.

P ublix Super Markets, based in Lakeland, FL, publishes a biweekly bulletin that lists the births, deaths, marriages and serious illnesses of employees and their families. For more than twenty years, the president sent personalized cards to the families of everyone listed in the bulletin.

At Tektronix, Inc., employees elect a representative from their work groups (one area
rep for about every forty employees). Once a
month, each work group is granted forty minutes
of paid company time for an area rep activity,
which the area rep organizes. Generally speak-
ing, area reps use the time to learn more about
different aspects of the company. They may visit
another Tektronix facility. They may visit a customer. They may visit a supplier. They may
invite a senior official to talk about a specific
subject.

Monthly, the approximately 300 area reps get
together for a forum on a topic of interest, such
as compensation. Employees throughout the
company submit questions for their area reps to
ask the executives who speak at such forums.
Once a year the area rep meeting is addressed by
the president, who delivers a State of Tektronix
speech. The tougher questions and the president's answers are reported in full in the next
issue of the company's weekly newsletter, "Tek-
week."

☛ *Present State of the*
Place reports periodically
to your employees,
acknowledging the work
and contributions of
individuals and groups.

Employees at Federal Express have a Guaranteed Fair Treatment (GFT) procedure in
which employees are encouraged to file
grievances if they believe they have not been
treated fairly. The procedure was developed
from a policy at Marriott Corporation. Managers
are also covered by the procedure. In one case, a
middle manager filed a GFT because she
thought she had been wrongly denied a promotion. A board of review found in her favor and

ordered that she receive a comparable promotion. Far from being penalized for using the GFT, two years later she was given a $5,000 award for outstanding service in her new management position.

———

66 Employees deserve to know what's up and will handle the responsibility better than you imagine. 99

—NANCY K. AUSTIN, Management Consultant

Time Off

O ne reward frequently given in most companies is time off. Whether it is a free day or a six-month sabbatical, this form of recognition is almost universally desired by employees.

In a recent survey conducted by Hilton Hotels Corporation, as reported in *Entrepreneur Magazine* in December 1991, 48 percent of 1,010 workers said they would give up a day's pay for an extra day off each week. If the reward were two days off, an additional 17 percent said they would consent to a one-day wage reduction. The responses differed somewhat by gender: 54 percent of working women would take a pay cut for extra time, as opposed to 43 percent of men.

There are three ways you can use time off as a reward, according to Michael LeBoeuf, author of *The Greatest Management Principle in the World:*

1. If the job permits it, simply give people a task and a deadline and specify the quality you expect. If they finish before the deadline, the extra time is their reward.

2. If the job is one where employees must be present all day, specify an amount of work you want done by a certain time. If the work is completed on time and satisfactorily, reward them with an afternoon, day or week off. Or you can set up a scoring system in which people earn an hour off for maintaining a certain output for a specific period. When they earn four hours, they can have a half day off; eight hours earns a day off, and so on.

3. Award time off for improvements in quality, safety, teamwork or any behavior you believe is important.

The Walt Disney Company grants an extra five-minute break (or a candy bar) to the employee who finds the guest who has traveled farthest to come to the park.

According to Michelle Gillis, sales manager of CareerTrack, an organizer of management seminars in Boulder, CO, the company gives an employee a half day off with pay if he or she recommends a person who is hired and makes it past the ninety-day probation period.

Cygna Group, an engineering and consulting firm in Oakland, has a Take the Rest of the Day Off and Do—— reward, according to Maureen Leland, director of corporate services. After finishing a big project, for example, a manager might spontaneously give the people involved the rest of the day off and take them to a ball game—often springing for tickets and beer.

Integrated Genetics, a biotechnology company in Boston, hosted a Ferris Bueller's Day Off. All employees were gathered for a business meeting—and then it was announced that instead of a meeting, they were going to have an all-day celebration. Skits were put on, movies shown (including *Ferris Bueller's Day Off*) and refreshments provided, including popcorn. Employees were encouraged to take a day off in the upcoming year to have fun.

☛ Provide an extra break.

☛ Give the person a two-hour lunch—and pay for dessert.

☛ Grant two-hour lunches for one week or for one day a week for one month.

☛ Grant a day off.

☛ Give the person a three-day weekend.

☛ Give spontaneous time off for specific accomplishments.

☛ Give the person a week off and arrange to have his or her work done.

Non-Monetary Rewards

- ✔ Weekend trips to resorts
- ✔ Time off
- ✔ Banquets
- ✔ Luncheons
- ✔ Tickets to local events
- ✔ Publicity (company and external)
- ✔ Certificates of recognition
- ✔ "Traveling" awards (monthly)
- ✔ Plaques
- ✔ Special parking spaces
- ✔ Free parking (in large cities)
- ✔ Shopping sprees
- ✔ Books, tapes or videos
- ✔ Family photo sessions
- ✔ Trophies
- ✔ Redeemable "Atta-boys/girls"
- ✔ Briefcases
- ✔ "Boss of the Day"

L innton Plywood Association in Portland, OR, offers extended personal leaves without pay. A foreperson can approve any leave less than thirty days, and the board of directors approves longer requests. Some workers take off several months a year. No requests have ever been turned down.

———

L evi Strauss & Company, headquartered in San Francisco, has a Quiet Room where an employee can take a solitary break to relax, pound on the walls, scream, meditate or read.

———

E mployees at Marion Laboratories in Kansas City, MO, take Friday afternoons off with pay during the summer in a program called Uncommon Days.

———

E mployees at Polaroid, based in Cambridge, MA, get to choose by vote one paid holiday a year in addition to the nine regular ones provided by the company.

———

A t Reader's Digest in Pleasantville, NY, employees work a thirty-five-hour week and may choose a flex-time schedule. There are typically twelve paid holidays and an additional five floating personal days.

———

R OLM Corporation, based in Santa Clara, CA, and the second-largest maker of telephone exchanges in the United States, offers the ultimate flex-time plan, allowing employees to work whenever they want to, subject to the approval of their immediate supervisor or work group.

A t Apple Computer in Cupertino, CA, all employees were granted an extra week's paid vacation when the company had its first $100-million sales quarter.

P epsiCo headquarters in Purchase, NY, has hired a full-time concierge to help its 800 employees with personal errands such as booking restaurant tables and theater seats, arranging events for children, and household repairs. The company started the service after a survey showed that employees had no free time for running such errands.

Other time-saving services the company has arranged include a dry cleaner in the headquarters building, a mobile oil-change service in the parking lot twice a month, a shoeshine man roaming the halls twice a week, and the selling of take-home dinners in the cafeteria every day at 4:30. They recently brought in a shoe repair service and hope soon to bring in a tailor for employees' use.

✔ President's Medallion

✔ Free meals (on-the-spot award)

✔ Cookouts

✔ Attendance at outside seminars or conferences

✔ Photo session with company president

✔ Popular company logo items (T-shirts, gym bags, coffee mugs, pen-and-pencil sets, jackets, stadium chairs, ice chests, umbrellas, thermos jugs, paper weights, desk pen sets, leather goods)

—K. H. "SKIP" WILSON,
Senior Training Specialist,
Mississippi Power
& Light Company

> ❝ Smart companies realize that helping workers, especially around a stressful time, is a very important part of good leadership. ❞
>
> —DR. ANN MCGEE-COOPER,
> Consultant

After seven years at Intel Corporation, a manufacturer of semiconductors, memories, computer systems and software in Santa Clara, CA, employees become eligible for eight weeks off, with full pay, on top of their regular three-week vacation. They may also apply for six months off, with pay, for public service, teaching or exceptional educational opportunities.

McDonald's offers a three-month sabbatical after ten years' service. At Moog Automotive, a St. Louis manufacturer of electrohydraulic control products, employees can take a seven-week vacation on their tenth anniversary, in addition to their regular three-week vacation. Another seven-week vacation benefit is awarded on each subsequent fifth anniversary. If employees don't want to take the time off, they can take payment instead. ROLM's sabbatical program offers any employee three months off at full pay after each six years of service. Company-paid sabbaticals are also available at Tandem Computers, where employees get six additional weeks for each four years of service. Time Warner offers a sabbatical after fifteen years—at half salary for at least three months and up to six months.

Cash/ Cash Substitutes/ Gift Certificates

Most people enjoy getting extra spending money—especially around the holidays. In a recent survey of American workers, 95 percent considered a cash bonus a positive and meaningful incentive. The only problem with giving cash is that often employees simply use the money to pay bills and quickly forget the reward.

Cash or cash substitutes (such as coupons or points that can be traded for products) do, however, give the employee flexibility in deciding how to use the reward. Since it is their choice, the likelihood of satisfaction increases. Gift certificates have the advantage of quick fulfillment and flexible dollar amounts and expiration dates, and carry no shipping costs. They can be redeemed in a wide variety of places for a broad range of merchandise, from gourmet food to lawn mowers.

Thomas J. Watson, Sr., founder of IBM, reportedly wrote checks on the spot to employees who were doing an outstanding job.

Lowell G. Rein, chairman of LGR Consultants in McMurray, PA, offers several ideas for rewards that involve relatively small amounts of cash:

> **❝ Cash is king. Then workers want benefits, bonuses, and incentives in that order. Workers want incentives in the form of salary, profit sharing, incentive travel, time off, perks, recognition and professional development. ❞**
>
> —BARRY GOODE,
> Director of Quality,
> IBM Canada

✔ Offer silver dollars or gold coins for good work, a good safety record or perfect attendance.

✔ Periodically give $20 bills to employees (or groups of employees) who excel.

✔ Place small cash awards with personal thank-you notes inside employees' calendars or desk drawers.

✔ Choose an outstanding employee to receive a small (but permanent) pay raise.

✔ Offer unexpected cash bonuses.

———

Each department at the Veterans Administration Philadelphia Regional Office and Insurance Center receives a number of $25 On-the-Spot-Awards, which managers give spontaneously to workers they believe go beyond the call of duty. To increase the visibility of award-winners' efforts, the office has also created a case displaying employees' plaques and certificates and internal newsletters citing award-winners and their actions.

———

Pitney Bowes, headquartered in Stamford, CT, awards a $25 savings bond for the best oral and written questions submitted at the annual stockholder's meeting.

———

Sandy Edwards, human resource representative for Great Western Drilling Company in Midland, TX, says the company offers a $25 savings bond to the employee who poses the most challenging question to the president at the company communication meetings. Great Western also hosts an employee appreciation banquet with a twist: Each employee receives $200 in play money to use at an auction. As part of the auction, managers take bids on services such as washing cars, baby-sitting, house-sitting, baking a cake, cooking a meal, and doing an employee's job for six hours. Employees also receive two gold pieces and a sit-down dinner at the banquet.

> 66 Economic incentives are becoming rights rather than rewards. 99
>
> —PETER F. DRUCKER, Author and Management Guru

At Celestial Seasonings, which packages herbal teas in Boulder, CO, every employee receives a $25 check on his or her birthday, a $50 check at Thanksgiving and a $100 check at Christmastime.

At 3M (Minnesota Mining and Manufacturing Company), headquartered in St. Paul, employees are allowed $100 cash to spend on any innovative idea or process related to their job without further approval.

At Delta Business Systems in Orlando, FL, a wide range of nonsales employees are offered cash for a variety of improvements in productivity. Secretaries and administrative assistants, for example, compete monthly for a $50 award for Most Valuable Associate; each dispatcher can earn up to $40 a month by scheduling preventive maintenance calls, and workers in the company's four warehouses can divide up to $400 every two months if they function smoothly as a team. One offer of $200 a quarter to accounts receivable employees to reduce the company's outstanding bills cut long-term receivables in half and saved the company $10,000 within six months.

———

At National Office Furniture in Jasper, IN, fake cash is awarded during meetings held to test product knowledge, says Larry Schrock, communications director. At the end of the meeting, employees use the money to bid for prizes. Tickets for college football games and the Grand Ole Opry are also given away to top performers. When a company-wide slogan contest was held, winning teams received jackets. Weekly, managers invite staff members to join them for dinner or refreshments.

———

Burger King rewards workers with cash when they recruit management-level employees. For finding entry-level workers, employees receive "burger bucks" redeemable for gift certificates from local stores.

———

During especially busy periods, Nucor Corporation, a steel manufacturer in Charlotte,

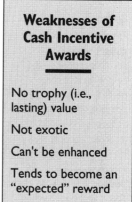
NC, goes to six-day workweeks, paying bonuses for the sixth day based on time-and-a-half pay.

_____

Steve Ettridge, president of Temps & Company, a temporary-employment service based in Washington, DC, had a problem with young workers who would not admit having done something wrong. "Most of the mistakes could have been fixed or minimized, but I never found out about them until they blew up," Ettridge says. "One day, I pulled out five hundred dollars in cash, and I told them about a mistake I'd made that week. I said that whoever could top it would get the money. Of course, they were afraid it was a trick." One employee finally admitted to a data-entry error that had caused a $2-million paycheck to be printed and almost mailed out. He got the $500. Since then the company gives out quarterly $100 awards to employees who admit mistakes they have made on the job. Ettridge says the award is designed to allow people to be human and to encourage risk-taking.

_____

At the Internal Revenue Service, cash awards of at least $100 are given for ideas (some go as high as $4,000). Workers who score well on their performance evaluations get cash bonuses averaging $500.

_____

Victor Kiam, president of Remington Products in Bridgeport, CT, maintains a $25,000

Weaknesses of Cash Incentive Awards

———

No trophy (i.e., lasting) value

Not exotic

Can't be enhanced

Tends to become an "expected" reward

> **❝** If you give a little recognition to your casual business acquaintances—the order-processing clerks, permit-review people, receptionists, et cetera—you'd be amazed to find out how much it means to them. I want our people to be able to see the people with whom they work. **❞**
>
> —JACK NOLAN, CEO, Nolan Scott

discretionary fund to give instant cash recognition to workers who have been spotted by their supervisors doing an exceptional job. Kiam calls these people to his office and hands out checks ranging from $200 to $500.

———

When an employee refers business that results in a sale for Gunneson Group International, a total quality consulting firm in Landing, NJ, he or she receives a cash award of 1 to 5 percent of the gross sale, depending on the value of the new business to the company.

———

G. S. Schwartz and Company Inc., a public relations firm in New York, holds a Hit Parade contest in which it awards $50 a week to the PR representative who demonstrates the best example of getting coverage of an event or generating a story for a client. The company also publishes a newsletter congratulating winners and highlighting their hits. Winners receive one point toward a $100 quarterly prize, and runners-up are awarded half a point.

———

The management consulting firm Goodmeasure, in Cambridge, MA, uses Atta Person Awards to say thank-you for above-and-beyond achievements—accompanied by on-the-spot awards of cash or gift certificates.

———

Quad/Graphics printing company in Pewaukee, WI, pays employees $30 to attend a seminar devoted to quitting smoking and gives $200 to anyone who quits for a year.

Grumman Corporation, an aerospace company based in Bethpage, NY, makes extensive use of Sears gift certificates for its employees. "With certificates, people can get whatever they want," says Marilyn Lage, senior buyer in the procurement department. "They might not always find something they like in an incentive merchandise catalog." In a recent year, Grumman has awarded more than 8,800 Sears gift certificates for $50 each.

Coupons worth $35 are given to employees at Wells Fargo Bank in San Francisco to be awarded to coworkers and peers for "extra effort" and "a job well done." The coupons are redeemable for gifts such as season tickets to a sporting event, a pedigreed puppy, five shares of company stock, Rose Parade tickets, shopping sprees, a one-month mortgage payment and paid days off.

Employees at the Naval Publications and Forms Center in Philadelphia nominate other employees for the Wilbur Award, named after a longtime employee, which comes with $25. Workers have the chance to earn a top award of $35,000 for an outstanding suggestion.

PUT YOUR MONEY WHERE YOUR HEART IS

☞ Offer a cash bonus with taxes prepaid.

☞ Send a $20, $50 or $100 bill to a spouse with a thank-you note for his or her support during the employee's overtime.

☞ Give employees who recruit new workers a cash bonus.

☞ Buy the person a gift certificate.

☞ Pay for the tutoring of an employee's child.

☞ Pay an employee's parking or traffic ticket.

☞ Pay an employee's mortgage for one month.

☞ Pay for a house-cleaning service for an employee's home.

Communication Briefings/Newstrack communication services in Blackwood, NJ, uses an Employee Recognition Coupon system that helps foster employees' appreciation of each others' contributions, more teamwork and better morale, reports PR director Gina Audio.

Each employee receives twenty coupons to distribute. When he or she sees a coworker doing anything extraordinary, he or she simply fills out a coupon with the reason for the recognition and gives it to the coworker. Employees save the coupons (to a maximum of twenty coupons per person per year) and redeem them for special awards:

1 coupon: certificate for free car wash

5 coupons: $25 gift certificate for dinner

10 coupons: $50 gift certificate for Macy's

15 coupons: one-night stay for two in Atlantic City

20 coupons: one-year membership to Four Seasons Health Spa

———

The Taylor Corporation, a printing company in North Mankato, MN, uses catalog selections instead of year-end bonuses, allowing employees to choose items they want.

———

American Express Company's "Be My Guest" plan treats an incentive-winner to dinner at the company's expense. The employee receives a certificate redeemable for a meal at a participating restaurant. The certificate charges the meal to the gift-giver's account; a preordained amount can be printed on the charge slip that accompanies the guest certificate.

———

The fibers department at E. I. du Pont de Nemours and Company in Wilmington, DE, has an Achievement Sharing program in which all employees put 6 percent of their salary at risk and are paid a sliding percentage of that amount based on how close their department comes to its annual goals. Less than 80 percent means no increase; 80 to 100 percent means a 3 to 6 percent increase; 101 to 150 percent means an increase of 7 to 19 percent.

———

When J. Pierpont Morgan, founder of the financial services holding company J. P. Morgan & Co., died in 1912 he bequeathed one year's salary to each member of his staff.

———

Solar Press, a direct-mail and packaging business based in Naperville, IL, has evolved a system of cash bonuses over the years. Initially cash bonuses were casual, even paternalistic. At the end of most months, founder John F. Hudetz would hand out checks—usually $20 to $60— with everyone getting the same amount.

> **"** Human beings need to be recognized and rewarded for special efforts. You don't even have to give them much. What they want is tangible proof that you really care about the job they do. The reward is really just a symbol of that. **"**
>
> —Tom Cash,
> Senior Vice President,
> Financial Services and
> Institutions Marketing
> and Sales,
> American Express

When the company reached $2 million in sales, the owners wanted to try a more clearly defined program. Employees were assigned to specific machines and divided into work teams of four or five; the more a team produced during a given month, the bigger the bonus for each member.

The new incentive system had an immediate effect. The packaging machines ran faster than ever as employees jockeyed for larger and larger payments. In many cases, production rates doubled. In good months, team members in the top group would see bonuses of about $250, while their counterparts might receive a quarter of that. Because of the pressure to produce, however, other problems occurred, such as machine breakdowns caused by a failure to carry out regular maintenance.

Now the company rewards everyone for bottom-line results according to the clear-cut formula: Every quarter, managers set a target for profitability based on what they think is within reach. Assuming the company meets the goal—and the numbers are openly discussed within the company—25 percent of the incremental earnings goes into a bonus pool. The pool is then divided in relation to a person's earnings during the previous quarter. If, for example, an employee earned 0.5 percent of the total payroll, he or she is entitled to 0.5 percent of the bonus pool, modified by two factors: It takes two years to become fully vested in the program, and unexcused absences or tardiness can shrink a check.

EVOLUTION OF SOLAR PRESS'S CASH INCENTIVE PROGRAM

INTERNAL BONUSES, COMPANYWIDE 1977–84

Upside: No promises, easy to administer
Downside: Employees didn't know what they were being rewarded for; no motivational effect

PRODUCTION BONUSES, BY TEAM 1984–88

Upside: Stimulated output and creativity
Downside: Set off rivalries among departments and individuals; created equipment and quality problems; administrative nightmare

PROFIT-SHARING BONUSES, COMPANYWIDE 1987–PRESENT

Upside: Simple to understand; emphasizes teamwork and interdepartmental coordination
Downside: More difficult for individuals to influence

Merchandise/ Apparel/Food

Many companies find giving merchandise to employees a very effective form of recognition, especially if the individuals have a choice in what they get. In a recent survey of American workers, 63 percent ranked merchandise incentives as meaningful.

Merchandise incentives are desirable and promotable, since a good selection can appeal to every taste and can be used to reward achievement at various levels and times. Such incentives have "trophy value"—they form a concrete reminder of past performance and also serve as a constant reminder that future performance will be rewarded. Items valued up to $400 for safety and length-of-service awards are tax-deductible to the company and are excluded from the employee's taxable income. Merchandise can be obtained at wholesale prices and can be drop-shipped. Finally, redemptions take place at the end of a program, so major costs are incurred after results are in. Merchandise incentives do have a couple of disadvantages: They require detailed administration and are inappropriate for participants who earn low wages.

The best merchandise for incentive campaigns has lasting value, reflects the quality of the recipient's achievements as well as the gratitude of the sponsoring company, inspires pride of ownership, is useful, suits the recipient's lifestyle and tastes, projects a positive image of the company, can be fulfilled promptly and without hassle, and is guaranteed and exchangeable.

Kirk Malicki, president of Pegasus Personal Fitness Centers in Dallas, asks new fitness trainers to make a list of rewards, ranging in value from $25 to $200, they would like to receive for reaching weekly and monthly goals. Instead of commonplace prizes, his fifteen employees have opted for tickets to rock concerts, limousine rentals and half days off. Thanks in part to the customized incentives, sales have more than doubled in six years. "They know what motivates them better than I do," Malicki says, "so I just ask."

———

Fred Maurer, sales manager of special markets at Canon USA in Lake Success, NY, believes that with merchandise, people can get more in value than the company actually spends. "Let's assume you give salespeople $100 for a 10 percent increase in sales and $200 dollars for a 20 percent increase," Maurer says. "If you can offer that salesperson a choice of three or four items that cost $100 at wholesale, he or she gets something worth more than if he or she had bought it at retail. This fact of life—that we offer people more for their money—is key to the incentive business, and it isn't publicized enough."

Maurer's preference in incentive merchandise is "anything to do with home offices, fax machines and home copiers in particular. These items are not only nice to have, but also help make people that much more efficient."

———

> 66 There's no knowing what any given employee will value as a reward. That's why, with noncash items, we recommend offering employees a wide range of rewards. Let them choose whatever is to their personal liking. 99
>
> —Barcy Fox,
> Vice President,
> Performance Systems,
> Maritz Motivation
> Company

Motivating Merchandise

Electronics—People love to own the latest gadgets: digital audio-tapes, VCRs, video cameras and compact disc players.

Productivity enhancements—Tools can help people improve their efficiency: fax machines, cellular phones, laptop computers.

Unique customized gifts—Customized gifts add special meaning: special-edition lithographs, antiques, company-imprinted credit cards (such as Visa or MasterCard).

Compact versions of old favorites—Space-saving appliances add value: compact washers and dryers; under-the-counter can openers, TVs and radios.

Services—Services help people save time: a housecleaner for a year, baby-sitting coupons, spa visits and facials.

The Hartford Steam Boiler Inspection and Insurance Company in Hartford, CT, spends up to $50 per year per administrative employee on gifts tailored to meet various employees' interests, including dinners for two, tickets to movies and sporting events, gift certificates, and coffee for a month. There are four criteria for an award: The employee must be a team player, take initiative to solve problems, provide leadership in supporting company goals, and show an attitude that inspires others to do their best. Spokesperson Karen Block says, "I believe that when the final results are in, the investment will be returned to us many times over."

Merchandise has a residual value over cash and even travel, says Bill Hicks, vice president of sales for special markets at Oneida Silversmiths in Oneida, NY, if only in the fact that "every time you look in your home at an item won through an incentive program, there's the knowledge of how it was won. I see it all the time; there's a story behind every incentive prize, whether it's merchandise or a trip."

Arthur Halloran, vice president of special market sales at Sony Corporation, agrees: "Despite the competitive prices available for electronic products, incentive merchandise in one's home indicates the accomplishment of winning."

Judy Yovanovich, public relations manager for the Florists' Transworld Delivery Asso-

ciation, based in Southfield, MI, reports that many firms arrange with florists to send flowers to employees on birthdays, on personal and company anniversaries and in the case of illness or death. Yovanovich says employers have also found that having flowers and plants in offices and on desks is great for morale.

"Flower power" is a growing promotional tool," Yovanovich says. Many businesses have found that they can effectively use flowers throughout the year. Some of the country's largest corporations have incorporated flowers into employee incentive programs or promotional programs for consumers.

Some companies have used flowers as prizes in proof-of-purchase coupon promotions. Others have used flowers as an incentive for company salespeople who meet quotas or for dealers as a token of appreciation for their business. Still others have used flowers as a thank-you gift to purchasers of big-ticket items.

Companies are attracted to flower and plant gifts because there is great variety to choose from, selections for any budget and no worries about people's taste, their size, wrapping or shipping. Perhaps best of all, flowers are considered one of the most thoughtful gifts, available to express many different emotions.

President Clinton sent a pink rose and a card signed by Hillary and himself to every White House staffer to commemorate the first 100 days that the administration was in office. The

LET THEM DECIDE

☛ Give the person a choice among several rewards.

☛ Buy the person something from a catalog of his or her choice.

☛ Buy the individual an outfit of his or her choice.

☛ Award coupons redeemable for a gift of his or her choice.

card said "Thanks for being part of the first 100 days." Seventy top officials received sterling-silver Tiffany key chains, each with a tiny silver saxophone attached.

———

At Citibank in Oakland, customers (and other employees) can reward and thank employees with Thumbs-Up certificates, which the recipient can exchange for merchandise. "Thumbs-Up is flashy and fun," says Charlene Belitz, employee reward and recognition programs manager. Early in the program, many workers were so pleased by the recognition the certificates stood for that instead of redeeming them immediately, they proudly displayed them on their walls.

———

Howard Henry, executive director of the Association of Incentive Marketing (AIM) in Union, NJ, believes that the ideal incentive program combines merchandise and travel. "Travel has a certain romantic aspect that's very nice," Henry says. "It's very appealing to be in a group that develops strong ties while on an incentive trip. On the other hand, merchandise is long-lasting." Henry believes the best impact is gained by combining the two so that "when you get to the travel portion of the program, you can use the merchandise there." He gives examples of matched luggage, an attaché case, skis, golf clubs or tennis rackets—anything that is relevant to the trip.

———

> 66 Merchandise works, but the challenge is to find the right product for your audience. We have four basic criteria for choosing merchandise awards: (1) The product must be of such high quality that it reflects positively on the company image; (2) it must be something everyone wants, preferably a state-of-the-art item that's on its way up in the consumer buying chain; (3) it must carry a high perceived value in relation to cost; and (4) its brand name must be instantly recognizable in a positive way. 99
>
> —Mark Weinberger,
> Marketing Service
> Manager,
> Cathay Pacific
> Airways Limited

As an exciting alternative to employees selecting merchandise from a catalog, some companies host shopping sprees, allowing award winners to go on a rampage through a warehouse that stocks appropriate prizes. Carlson Marketing Group has opened its Dayton, OH, distribution center to employees of Mobil, Toyota and Nabisco.

Carlson marketers fly their employees to Dayton for a pre-spree party the night before the appointed date. On the day of the event, employees walk the winners through the warehouse, pointing out where the most valuable goods are. The 200,000-square-foot warehouse contains about 4,500 items, including electronics, glassware, golf clubs and vacuum cleaners. Once winners are familiar with the layout, they can determine the quickest route to the items of most interest to them, according to Michael Barga, Carlson's director of distribution in Dayton.

Carlson recommends that sponsors limit the run-through to two minutes. "More than two minutes becomes a struggle for the participant, who's dashing down the aisles and throwing items into a big shopping cart," Barga says. On average, winners accumulate about $3,500 worth of goods per minute.

───────

Chevron USA, headquartered in San Francisco, keeps a large box, secured with a padlock, brimming with all sorts of gifts. An employee being recognized on the spot for some accomplishment is brought to the Treasure Chest by

> 66 I don't like cash because the cost-value relationship is one to one; I don't use travel because when dealers win, they have to use their vacation time to take the trip. Incentive travel can be self-defeating if it's a 'must' vacation. Merchandise, on the other hand, has a high perceived value and lots of flexibility. You must be sure to put quality into every decision, however. Don't cut corners on promotion or merchandise. With premiums, there is a very thick line between junk and quality 99
>
> —ROD TAYLOR,
> Group Promotion
> Manager of Paper
> Products,
> Procter & Gamble

his or her supervisor, who holds the keys. The employee gets to choose an item from the box: a coffee mug, pen-and-pencil set, gift certificate, coupon for lunch or dinner, or movie tickets. Recognition can come from supervisors and peers.

The Stone Container Corporation in Chicago topped a profitable year in which it gave every employee a television set, with the next profitable year, in which each employee received a VCR—24,000 in all were distributed. To announce the gift, the company made a ten-minute video with two actors impersonating Roger Ebert and Gene Siskel of TV's *At the Movies*. The characters reviewed the company's year, and footage of the various facilities was shown. Chief executive officer Roger Stone then appeared, gave the two-thumbs-up sign that Siskel and Ebert use when they like a movie, and announced the gift. At the end of the presentation, each employee received a certificate resembling a movie ticket, which was used to claim the VCR.

In Mary Kay Cosmetics' Career Apparel Program, sales consultants who reach specific goals become eligible to buy specific outfits for their wardrobes. Once someone qualifies to become a director, for example, she is invited to attend Mary Kay's management conference and, while there, is fitted for a director's suit, which she buys at the cost to the company. The style changes every year. Laura Whittier, manager of incentive merchandising says, "Our directors love the suits because they are functional and provide a visual symbol of their success. Qualifying to buy the suit indicates high status; wearing it results in a more professional look and instant recognition of success."

Flight attendants choose from a variety of uniform styles at Delta Airlines.

Shirley Kauppi, owner and manager of the King Copper Motel in Copper Harbor, MI, provides juice and pop, fruit and snacks to the cleaning staff. Kauppi also allows spouses and children to use one motel room to watch TV or read until the employees' work is done.

"Everyone eats," says Rick Farone, product and program coordinator for Royal Appliance, based in Cleveland. "When you reward people with food, you know it's something they'll use. Food makes people happy." An almost infinite variety of food gifts can be used to reward employees, including fruit baskets; fruit-of-the-month clubs; home-delivered steaks, seafood or lobster; jellies and jams; and spices.

D.D.B. Needham Worldwide, the advertising agency located in New York City, gives bottles of champagne to employees who go beyond the call of duty in developing an idea.

> 66 One reason food is a good motivator is that it provides the winner with an experience he or she can share with family and friends. Food is a social gift. 99
>
> —JEFFREY GIBEAULT, Sales Manager, Business Incentive Department, Omaha Steaks International

> **"** If someone takes you out for a fantastic dinner or cooks you something at home, you remember it for years. **"**
>
> —BOB VIDMAR,
> Manager,
> Sugardale Foods Inc.

☞ *Arrange for two Maine lobsters to be flown in for an employee and his or her spouse.*

Julie Milner, trainer for Servco Pacific, Inc., a diversified sales company in Honolulu, recommends giving employees gift certificates from a favorite restaurant, theater or clothing store. On particularly hectic days, she buys pizza for front-line employees as a recognition of their hard work.

———

At the Angus Barn Restaurant in Raleigh, NC, anytime an employee is "caught in the act of caring," he or she gets a choice of an entree from the restaurant's menu.

———

Recognition Items/Trophies/ Plaques

Recognition items are similar to general merchandise except that the items are customized for the individual, company or event, making them potentially more valuable as motivators, since they can serve for some time as reminders of the achievement or event.

In a recent survey of subscribers to *Personnel Journal,* almost two-thirds said they include plaques and certificates in their awards programs. Almost 15 percent give cash awards and 2 percent give savings bonds. More than 50 percent use jewelry, and 41 percent use watches.

Merchandise of any type is used by 41 percent of the organizations surveyed. Rings—along with travel—seem to constitute an integral part of sales incentive programs. Another 11 percent indicated they use travel incentives, and 17 percent said they give sales incentives in general. Trophies are awarded by 12 percent, ribbons by 2 percent.

According to a recent poll, the imprintable goods people most appreciate are clothing (T-shirts, jackets and caps), desk or office accessories, writing instruments, glassware and ceramics (including mugs), and calendars.

The travelers polled were also asked to name the most unusual imprinted product they had ever received, according to Specialty Advertising Association International, sponsor of the survey. Among their most interesting answers were a flyswatter, flower seeds, a broom holder, a rock, underwear, an athletic supporter, a brick, and a scarf from an Elvis impersonator.

> 66 I've come to the conclusion that there's no such thing as a bad cap program. Caps always go over really well, as do T-shirts, jackets and sweats. People seem to take great pride in displaying their company name and logo on their clothes. 99
>
> —JIM TURNER,
> Director of Safety
> and Loss Prevention,
> ANR Freight System

Employees of the Los Angeles Dodgers receive the same gifts and promotional items—Dodger caps, jackets, bats—that are given to fans during the baseball season.

———

David Walling, training coordinator for the Soil Conservation Service in Champaign, IL, reports using "spot awards"—specially designed coffee mugs, watches and pen-and-pencil sets. He also gives people special framed prints of wildlife or other subjects, depending on the person's preferences.

———

The City of Decatur gave each employee a "company jacket" with the city's logo on the front, according to Susan Nordquist, personnel specialist for the city.

———

Bill Nesbit, vice president of Quality Systems for Central Telephone Company of Illinois, tells two recognition stories. After a heavy ice storm, five workers were sent out to do overnight repairs on Valentine's Day. As a form of thanks, each employee's spouse was sent a box of chocolates with a card expressing the company's appreciation for her husband's efforts.

In another instance, heavy water damage to telephone cables took more than forty-nine people to set straight. The supervisor sent each a lottery ticket with a note that said, "I never gamble when I count on you."

Nesbit notes that both stories are significant because the company's past culture had made managers overly cautious in recognizing employees for fear of overlooking someone or of having to recognize too many people.

The Houghton Mifflin Company in Boston, as well as other publishers, customizes books to fit specific occasions. Books can be customized in several ways:

✔ Have the CEO personalize a book with an inscription to commemorate an occasion or achievement.

✔ Incorporate a company's logo on the front or back cover, or on the spine.

✔ Alter a book's title to feature a brand or a company. Warner Books, for instance, changed *How to Talk to Your Cat* to *The Meow Mix Guide to Cat Talk.*

✔ Insert product allusions into a book's text. For example, in a pet-care book a manufacturer could alter the sentence "Veterinarians recommend giving a dog food that is high in protein" to "Veterinarians recommend giving a dog food that is high in protein, such as Brand X." Book publishers note that usually this is possible only on large orders and when the product is appropriate to the text.

✔ Feature a letter or brief message from a company on a separate page before the title page.

> 66 Simple observation suggests that most of us are trinket freaks—if they represent a genuine thanks for a genuine assist. 99
>
> —TOM PETERS,
> Author and
> Management Consultant

☛ Give a token—a specially designed coin, for example—that can be redeemed for a future favor.

☛ Purchase a unique pen to serve as a memento for a task well done.

☛ Award a Gold Banana pin for an outstanding achievement.

☛ Design and present a plaque commemorating an achievement.

PERSONALIZE IT

☞ Award *personalized gifts that recognize distinctive interests or hobbies to all those involved with an innovation.*

☞ Give a *personalized company coffee cup or belt buckle.*

☞ Have a *pen-and-pencil set engraved for the person.*

☞ Personalize the label *on a wine bottle with a message of thanks for an achievement.*

☞ Have a *personalized cartoon made for an employee award. Comic Arts of Wilton, CT, can include the recipient's name, a team pennant, a sports picture and a customized caption in a cartoon.*

✔ Excerpt an appropriate chapter from an original work and create an entirely new book.

———

At Christmas, Blanchard Training and Development in Escondido, CA, gives all employees practical items such as a tire gauge, pocket flashlight, Swiss Army knife, emergency care packet for home or car, desk clock and picture frames—all inscribed with the company's logo, the employee's name, or both.

———

FIVE WAYS TO CUSTOMIZE AN APPAREL AWARD

1. Design an eye-catching graphic featuring your company name, logo or popular product name and place it prominently on the apparel.

2. Opt for a more subtle placement by sewing a tag with your name or logo onto a sleeve or cuff.

3. Create a special label to appear inside the cap or garment.

4. Place a crest with your logo on the pocket of a shirt, using a color slightly darker than that of the shirt.

5. For loyal long-term employees, offer a very high-quality brand-name item without your company name or logo, and present it with a

special card conveying your sincere appreciation for their hard work and support.

———

Rocky Laverty, president of the discount store chain Smart & Final in Los Angeles, awards "Rocky Dollars" for outstanding performance to employees, reports Curtis A. Skowronek, manager of human resource development. The award consists of a silver dollar mounted on a certificate, presented personally by the president with public congratulations.

———

The Sterling Optical Company, based in Woodbury, NY, awards savings bonds, certificates and plaques to employees for hitting branch sales targets and for outstanding service to customers and to the branch.

———

Recognition items can be generated around a theme such as "summer." Towels, umbrellas, rafts, chairs and coolers work well as standard promotional beach items. For a barbecue theme, options include grills, cooking utensils, hats and aprons—even a custom-built barbecue pit and patio furniture. Floats, boats and inner tubes can also be customized; for larger prizes, companies can use canoes and dinghies. Among recent users of such items are Pepsi, Columbo frozen yogurt, Sunkist soda and Moosehead beer.

———

Unusual Specialty Items

✔ Boxer shorts

✔ "Mick Jagger" lips alarm clock

✔ Jalapeño lollipops

✔ Portable picnic table and benches

✔ Spanish-speaking calculator

✔ Desktop toy train

✔ Coffee cup imprinted with a message that appears—or disappears—when the cup is filled

☞ Make "achievement" decals, badges or emblems for uniforms, hard hats, T-shirts, etc.

☞ Give promotional items such as safety buttons, bumper stickers and posters.

> 66 Incentive awards are not compensation—they are recognition—a meaningful way to say thank you, while focusing attention on your company goals. Incentive awards are recognition for a job well done, a personal expression of gratitude. They must carry a hassle-free guarantee of satisfaction. 99
>
> —THE MBF GROUP, INC.

Northern Telecom telecommunications in Richardson, TX, commissioned an original limited-edition sculpture by the Kirk Stieff Company to recognize the exceptional achievement of its Honor Circle winners. Pins, award certificates and travel prizes, as well as a theme video, a program brochure, posters and promotional mailings, complemented the merchandise campaign. Of 12,000 people eligible to participate in the program, 534 (34 percent more than expected) achieved their sales goals, and the company outdid its previous year's performance with a 13.4 percent boost in sales and a 3 percent increase in market share.

Fun/ Celebrations

Most employees would prefer to work in a fun environment in which they can enjoy their jobs and their coworkers. A fun environment includes specific celebrations for specific achievements and results. If you can reward a person and have fun in the process, you will satisfy two important desires of most employees: to be appreciated for the work they do and to enjoy their jobs and workplace.

At Minnesota-based Wilson Learning Corporation, each employee is given a Mickey Mouse watch after three months of employment as a reminder always to have fun while working for the company. On the tenth anniversary, the employee is given a gold Mickey Mouse watch.

Hewlett-Packard Company in Palo Alto, CA, uses informal beer busts in the afternoons to mark special events.

At Dow Corning, in Midland, MI, management hosted an ice-cream social at which managers made and served sundaes to their employees to thank them for an accomplishment, reports George K. Stevenson, human resources specialist.

> **66 If you want to thrive and remain competitive in a work that is changing radically and relentlessly, you need the fluidity and flexibility of humor. 99**
>
> —C.W. METCALF,
> President,
> C.W. Metcalf & Company

☛ *Ask a friend of the employee to suggest a gift or activity the employee might enjoy.*

☛ *Plan a roast of the person at a company meeting.*

☛ *Give employees Post-it notepads with sayings appropriate to their personalities.*

Merle Norman Cosmetics in Los Angeles buys its female employees a makeover for fun and to enhance their professional image.

———

Bank of America in San Francisco has a Laugh-A-Day Challenge for one month. Each employee tries to make coworkers laugh every day with cartoons and jokes. Winners receive T-shirts and books containing the best jokes and cartoons.

———

Matt Weinstein of PlayFair, a Berkeley, CA, company that offers humor seminars, suggests several ways to keep the work environment fun:

✔ Give your employees a casual dress day such as Hawaiian Day or Suspender Friday.

✔ Have a surprise picnic for your employees in the parking garage or parking lot.

✔ Make campaign buttons out of employees' baby pictures. Have them wear each other's buttons and try to figure out who's who.

✔ Put rubber fish in the water cooler.

✔ Staple Kleenex to potentially stressful memos.

✔ Glue chocolate kisses to boring memos.

Ritch Davidson, "senior vice emperor" at the company, adds:

✔ Issue a Laugh-A-Day Challenge to your staff. Ask everyone to bring in a joke or cartoon every day for a month; all who participate get a small prize. Print a booklet containing the submissions and distribute it to the staff.

✔ Designate days when anyone who makes a negative comment forks over a small sum of money—twenty-five or fifty cents—and use the money to start a Fun Committee fund.

✔ Thank people by giving chocolate kisses, balloons or other small items.

✔ Give employees ten-minute "joybreaks" during which they can do something fun (listen to a comedy tape, look at cartoons), and create a Joybreak Committee to plan occasional group activities.

✔ Instead of giving out holiday bonuses in checks, give out cash, close a few hours early and take everyone to a shopping mall. After the spree, stage a show-and-tell.

✔ Hold occasional fun contests—Nerf basketball or volleyball, bubble-blowing competitions—or play cooperative games such as charades and treasure hunts.

✔ Have a party for no reason at all.

———

D on Coyhis describes how a humor seminar helped when he was district manager for Digital Equipment Corporation's Colorado customer support center: "We taught everyone to juggle beanbags; if employees felt uptight after a call, they were encouraged to juggle to break the

> 66 Small things work, even seemingly corny things like putting cartoons above your desk or having everyone bring in pictures of themselves from the sixties. You don't have to be a comedian to display a light touch. 99
>
> —MALCOLM KUSHNER, President, Malcolm Kushner and Associates

☛ Provide tickets to a sporting, musical or cultural event, depending on the employee's preference.

☛ At an employee meeting, tape gift certificates to the bottom of chairs in the first three rows.

66 There is a great
creative void in
most of corporate
America. When you
inject a level of
humor and playful-
ness, employees find
a common ground.
They're reminded
that they're all
working on the same
side. 99

—CARL ROBINSON,
Vice President,
Organizational
Psychologists

tension and prepare for the next call. We also
instituted a Grouch Patrol, which was empowered to tell grouchy people to take a break. We
found that if we systematically took breaks, productivity improved."

A physical therapist's office instituted a Margarita Award for the therapist who had to
work with the toughest client that week or
month. The awardee was treated by the group to
a margarita happy hour.

Southwest Airlines, based in Dallas, runs contests for the fun of it, such as a Halloween
costume contest, a Thanksgiving poem contest
and a design contest for the December newsletter. The firm also has an annual chili cook-off.

Advanta Corporation, a financial services
firm in Horsham, PA, has its senior managers host a Grill Your Boss cookout at which
they dress up as chefs and cook hamburgers and
hot dogs for all employees, says Joan Cawley,
director of human resources.

The morning after a product passed a crucial
test at Odetics, a mariachi band paraded
through the plant, followed by clerks from the
local Baskin-Robbins franchise offering free ice
cream.

Blanchard Training and Development in Escondido, CA, celebrates a Day of Excellence once a year with fun and learning activities for all employees. Managers use the day to host a Murder Mystery, hand out personality tests or have a hypnotist entertain. One manager hires a masseuse to give his workers shoulder and neck massages on Valentine's Day. The same person has employees in his department randomly select a day during the year that becomes their "special day." Managers plan fun activities for individuals during lunch or in the late afternoon of that day.

———

First Chicago, a bank holding company, gives out Felix and Oscar Awards to the employees with the neatest and messiest work areas.

———

At a recent quarterly meeting, Apple Computer executives in Cupertino, CA, used kazoos instead of applause to indicate their approval of speakers.

———

At the corporate offices of Domino's Pizza in Ann Arbor, MI, everyone from the president to the receptionist wears a red, white and blue Domino's uniform once a week. Employees are invited to bring their pets to work on Fridays.

———

RESEARCH THEIR FAMILY

☞ *Provide a family history. Family Connection traces the history of family names. The information is presented on a twelve-by fourteen-inch certificate made of parchment-tone paper. "We write up all the key details in the history of a surname, and the information dates back to when it was first recorded in writing," says Martin O'Shea, president of the company. "Aside from telling where the name originates and what it means, we can document famous people who have the same name and provide family coats of arms where available." The company has a computer data base of over 300,000 surnames.*

☞ *Coordinate a surprise celebration of the achievements of an employee or group of employees.*

> **❝ I think it's impor-
> tant to have fun at
> work—and not just
> at holiday time. ❞**
>
> —ELLEN JACKOFSKY,
> Assistant Professor,
> Southern Methodist
> University

At Eastman Kodak in Rochester, NY, an executive formed a Humor Task Force to gather Monty Python videos, Woody Allen books, plastic chattering teeth and other props for a "Humor Room."

———

Liebert Corporation in Columbus, OH, which manufactures air-conditioning and power-supply systems for computer rooms, offers free popcorn to employees all day long.

———

Children's Hospital/King's Daughters Corporation in Norfolk, VA, hosts a stress-relief fair for employees with booths (dunk tank, Velcro dartboards, massage booths) and food.

———

Parties are always breaking out at Time Warner in New York. For example, when *Money* magazine moved from the twenty-ninth to the thirty-third floor of the Time & Life Building in Rockefeller Center, the staff held a block party. The best employee parties are reportedly held at Time Warner, Advanced Micro Devices, Apple Computer, Leo Burnett, Hewlett-Packard, Odetics and Tandem Computers.

———

EASY OFFICE MORALE BOOSTERS

1. Order pizza or a huge submarine sandwich for a communal lunch.

2. Designate a bulletin board as a place for employees to post favorite jokes, cartoons, etc.

3. Attach cartoons or humorous anecdotes to the more mundane memos that need to be circulated.

4. Schedule a staff meeting off-site in a congenial atmosphere; if possible, follow up with a casual social event.

5. Schedule an Ugly Tie (or Crazy Sweater or Silly Socks) Day with a joke prize for the winner.

6. Hold betting pools for such high-profile events as the Super Bowl, the Kentucky Derby, the Oscars, the Emmys and the World Series.

7. Take a daily humor break; designate someone to share a joke or funny story with the rest of the staff.

8. During a lunch break, screen a funny film or television show in a conference room or large office.

9. Bring a Polaroid camera to work. Take candid shots of employees and post the results throughout the office.

66 We spend an extraordinary amount of time just worrying about the environment and the people in it. 99

—LEWIS T. PRESTON,
Chairman,
J. P. Morgan

☛ *Let employees take a Dream Day to go to the beach and contemplate job, life and future. Ask them to report any insights when they return.*

10. Make it a point to smile and say hello to office mates.

11. Give everyone an opportunity to arrive an hour late or leave an hour early one day a week.

12. Never take anything too seriously. Keep reminding yourself, "This isn't brain surgery." (Unless, of course, it *is* brain surgery.)

———

Merle Norman Cosmetics sponsors an Employee Night every other Saturday at the San Sylmar container manufacturing facility located in the San Fernando Valley outside Los Angeles. First-run movies are shown for employees, who may bring as many as six friends. After the movie, employees and their guests can make their own free ice-cream sundaes.

———

Marion Laboratories, Inc., in Kansas City, MO, takes all of its employees and their spouses or guests (some 2,500 people) to see the Kansas City Royals play baseball once a year. Everyone wears a baseball cap or T-shirt with a big M on it, and top executives of the company go up and down the aisles handing out free drinks and other refreshments.

———

At the Space Camp in Cannes, France, employees can train much the way astronauts do, learning about satellite deployment, aerodynamics and astronomy as well as working in simulated weightlessness and training in other space environments such as hypergravity. The program culminates in a simulated space flight. French operations of Microsoft and Aerospatiale, a manufacturer of airplanes, satellites and missiles, both sent employees to Space Camp.

———

Linda L. Miles, president of Linda L. Miles & Associates, a seminar-planning firm in Virginia Beach, VA, treated her staff of six women to a pedicure in an award that came to be called Happy Feet Day.

———

Odetics, Inc., has its own Fun Committee, which launched Project Girth. For every pound an employee lost, a dollar would be sent to his or her favorite charity. Odetics also sponsored a Guess the Stock Price on March 31 contest in which the winner got a free lunch at the Hoagie Bar in Santa Ana. The plant's conference room has an exact replica of the space shuttle *Columbia* made out of Budweiser beer cans.

———

IBM, Coca-Cola, Ford, Monsanto and Nikon all purchase gold-sealed Star Certificates declaring employees' ownership of actual stars, with a star album containing a sky chart and star verification record. Star certificates are available for $45 from the International Star Registry in Ingleside, IL.

———

> ❝ I prefer things that are spontaneous. Things I hate the most are the routine, expected things like an annual company picnic. I think it's important for there to be an element of humor, laughter. It adds to the company. It's one more thing that makes you want to get up in the morning and go to work. ❞
>
> —JOEL SLUTZKY,
> Chairman,
> Odetics, Inc.

66 I've been reading literature on psychology for as far back as twenty-five years, and everything I've read says incentives are an effective way to tap a worker's intrinsic motivation, his inherent desire to do a job well. **99**

—TOM PETERS,
Author and
Management Consultant

First Pennsylvania Bank in Philadelphia arranges a once-a-year banquet for employees (and their families) who "take that extra step."

Employees at Blanchard Training and Development in Escondido, CA, get two movie passes on their birthdays.

Employees pick random birthdays and provide a cake and celebration at Windsor Shirt Company.

When four employees had birthdays on the same day at Porterville Developmental Center in Porterville, CA, coworkers blindfolded them and drove them to a restaurant, putting signs on their backs that read, "It's my party," and everyone in the restaurant stood and sang "Happy Birthday."

At the Spaceborne plant of Odetics, everybody's picture appears on a huge hanging calendar on his or her birth date.

According to Karen Evans Smith, vice president and manager of training and development for Central Bank of the South in Birmingham, AL, the bank plans a lunch outing for each person's birthday. The person whose birthday it is gets to select the restaurant, and the

manager personally picks up the tab. All other staffers are invited to attend on a "Dutch treat" basis.

———

H.B. Fuller Company, maker of adhesives, glues and sealants in St. Paul, and Recreational Equipment, Inc., (REI) in Seattle give employees the day off on their birthdays. Lowe's Companies, a lumber and hardware supply retailer headquartered in North Wilkesboro, NC, offers them a free lunch, and all Mary Kay Cosmetics employees receive a birthday card and a voucher for a lunch for two.

———

Spouses of employees at the Black & Decker Corporation in Anaheim, CA, get flowers on the employee's birthday, thanking them for their support, reports Bill Paolillo, district manager for the Western Region. Flowers also go to the spouses of employees who travel extensively, to show appreciation for the sacrifice.

———

The president of Merle Norman Cosmetics keeps track of everyone's birthday and when possible makes a point of seeking out people to wish them well on that day. The company chef also bakes a birthday cake for the employee.

———

At the Veterans Administration Philadelphia Regional Office and Insurance Center,

> 66 Staff birthday bashes are more common than board meetings. When your big day comes, we round everyone up and sing 'Happy Birthday' to you. We do this for everyone. 99
>
> —HARVEY MACKAY, President, Mackay Envelope Corp.

☞ *Coordinate a surprise celebration of the achievements of an employee or group of employees.*

☞ *Have an appreciation and welcome party whenever an employee leaves or joins your work unit.*

during the month of his or her birthday, each employee has the privilege of giving a coworker the office's Extra Step Award, a $30 cash prize for employees who go out of their way to satisfy their internal customers.

———

On a person's birthday at San Diego-based software developer Four Pi Systems, coworkers individually delivered a single flower every fifteen minutes throughout the day.

———

Personal letters and cards are sent from headquarters in Enfield, CT, to the stores of Dairy Mart, marking people's birthdays and wedding anniversaries.

———

A CASE STUDY IN RECOGNITION

In the Electro-Optics Division of Honeywell Inc., headquartered in Minneapolis, financial difficulties were causing a serious dip in morale that was leading to additional problems. The company needed to turn the situation around, but had to do so on a very low budget, given the state of the division. Seeking a creative solution, managers developed a recognition program titled Great Performers. "The division was looking for top performance from its employees," says Deborah van Rooyen, program director, "and that got me thinking that top performance comes from top performers, and that got me

thinking about top performers everyone is familiar with."

Van Rooyen spent a month in the local library researching the lives of great performers in politics, education, social work, business, science and the arts. All the people she studied had one characteristic in common: They succeeded by overcoming obstacles.

Van Rooyen's idea was to put together a program in which these people's well-known accomplishments would be celebrated alongside those of division employees. In theory, the possibility of being named a Great Performer would inspire employees to put forth their best effort.

"Turnaround begins with small accomplishments," van Rooyen says, "so we wanted to convey the idea that every job is important. For example, we wanted to encourage secretaries to type a letter only once, and to encourage employees in the shipping department to be careful enough that nothing would get broken, and so forth."

Management accepted the idea, and van Rooyen worked with the division's staff to finalize the list of forty celebrity Great Performers, being careful to include men, women, minorities, teams and historical figures.

A teaser campaign then followed featuring the celebrity Great Performers with memorable quotes. Employees were invited to nominate Great Performers, and were asked to explain the reasons for their nomination. A committee of volunteers reviewed the nominees. All were given pins in the shape of the letter G (for great) and the committee selected five employees they

> **"** Pay geared to performance is important, but so is 'rah-rah.' **"**
>
> —DANIEL FINKELMAN,
> Principal,
> McKinsey & Company

thought best exemplified the spirit of the program. The winning employees were interviewed,
and stories were created to use on posters that
looked just like the ones featuring the celebri-
ties. Each included the employee's photo, a
quote and copy describing the employee's
achievements and contributions.

"The posters were a visible way to help boost
self-esteem," says Chuck Madaglia, division
public relations manager. "The idea was to catch
employees doing something right and get them
feeling good about themselves."

The response was overwhelmingly positive.
The Great Performers became corporate celebri-
ties overnight, and everyone wanted to be one.
Many more individuals had the chance: Five
new employees were selected each month during
the year the program was in place. Morale
improved dramatically, and the ongoing program
encouraged employees to make changes in work
habits, make successful proposal bids, begin
recycling scrap and improve quality control.
Within six months, the division was in the black,
thanks in part to the success of the program.

PART II

AWARDS FOR SPECIFIC ACHIEVEMENTS AND ACTIVITIES

Many companies seek to tailor rewards to specific achievements or behaviors. Most of these rewards recognize employee achievements that are desired in organizations everywhere, such as cost-saving suggestions, exceptional customer service and the attainment of sales goals.

The Lincoln Electric Company in Cleveland is considered one of the first U.S. companies to establish an incentive program for its employees. In 1914 management set up an advisory board of elected representatives from each department. The board has met every two weeks ever since. The program the board devised was based on the following principles and practices:

✔ Holding individuals accountable for quality and output.

✔ Tying wages and bonuses directly to quality and output.

✔ Staffing departments exactly to cut absenteeism and emphasize the importance of each employee's job.

✔ Maintaining the fewest possible layers of management.

Lincoln's innovative practices have come to be commonplace throughout all industries in organizations that are serious about obtaining the highest productivity and performance possible. In this section are numerous examples of such programs.

Outstanding Employee Awards

O ne award found in most organizations is the Outstanding Employee or the Employee of the Month. This type of reward can be based on a variety of criteria, both informal and formal, and can be given for a single exceptional achievement or a great number of praiseworthy activities. The award is all the more meaningful when it involves selection by one's peers, not just by management.

A t Home Depot, Inc., the home improvement supply centers headquartered in Atlanta, each store picks an Employee of the Month, someone who has given time to an area of the store that technically lies outside his or her responsibility. The honoree gets $100, a merit badge (collecting five badges earns an extra $50) and a special badge to wear on his or her apron. The employee's name is also engraved on a plaque at the front of the store.

> 66 Brains, like hearts, go where they are appreciated. 99
>
> —ROBERT MCNAMARA, Former U.S. Secretary of Defense

A t ICI Pharmaceuticals Group in Wilmington, DE, the Performance Excellence Award is given to employees for any idea that helps the business (saving money, increasing productivity, etc.) or to employees who go "above and beyond" the call of duty, says Deb-

☛ Host Employee of the Month awards for highest productivity, quality or sales; most improvement; least absenteeism, or whatever you designate as most important. Display a photo of the employee in a prominent place, and honor him or her throughout the month at a series of lunches or other events.

bie Newkirk, training coordinator. The award winner receives $300. A person can be nominated for this award by anyone: a peer, supervisor, coworker or department head.

———

Once a month at Meridian Travel Inc. in Cleveland, CEO Cynthia Bender has the company's sixty-two employees write in their vote for Employee of the Month. "Managers always have their favorites, but the employees know who pitches in and helps out," says Bender. "It's important that different departments don't become isolated. This makes employees notice others more and develops camaraderie."

———

The Golden Falcon Awards at Federal Express in Memphis include a gold uniform pin, a congratulatory phone call from a senior executive and ten shares of stock (recently worth about $45 a share).

———

At Gregerson's Foods, a retail grocery chain in Cadsden, AL, outstanding employees are named Associates of the Month at each store location. They receive a silver name tag inscribed with that title, with the month and year of the award, to wear as long as they work for the company. This award is a highly prized possession, says Beverly McAlister, benefits administrator. The employees' names are also listed on plaques at each store.

———

Managers at D'Agostino's, a supermarket chain based in New Rochelle, NY, name employees All-Stars when they go beyond the call of duty. At least one All-Star is chosen each month from each store, up to twenty-four people per year per store.

———

At the Unitog Company, a leading maker of industrial uniforms and business clothing based in Kansas City, MO, top executives visit each plant to present the Wonder Worker Award, as nominated by coworkers. The Wonder Worker of the Year at each location receives cash, a personalized plaque that remains on view at the plant for the entire year and a crystal trophy with the Unitog logo embedded inside. A typical award for a quarterly winner might be a Unitog sweater and a day off with pay.

———

Blue Cross/Blue Shield Association, based in Chicago, gives People Are Tops Awards, which include balloons tied to the person's desk, belly dancers, and a song or message delivered by a person in a gorilla suit. The company also recognizes outstanding employees four times a year with Superstar Awards. Each Superstar gets a $500 savings bond, a star and a sweatshirt.

———

At the annual profit-sharing banquet, management at the Angus Barn Restaurant in Raleigh, NC, gives out achievement awards to the top ten all-around best employees. The

> **High achievers love to be measured, when you come down to it, because otherwise they can't prove to themselves that they are achieving.**
>
> —DR. ROBERT N. NOYCE,
> Cofounder,
> Intel Corporation

☞ *Create a special award for specific major accomplishments and name it (a Gorilla Award, for example).*

☞ *Create an ABCD (Above and Beyond the Call of Duty) Award for employees who exceed the requirements of their jobs. Give them a polo shirt emblazoned with "ABCD Award."*

☞ *Have employees vote for the top Manager, Supervisor, Employee and Rookie of the Year.*

☞ *Dedicate the parking space closest to the company entrance to the outstanding Employee of the Month.*

restaurant also has an award called the People's Choice Award; given by coworkers, it recognizes the model employee, best team player, etc.

———

Wal-Mart Stores, Inc., headquartered in Bentonville, AR, offers extensive award programs such as Regional All-Star Teams, the Special Divisions' All-Star Departmental Honor Roll, the VPI (Volume Producing Item) Contest, the Department Sales Honor Roll and the Shrinkage Incentive Program. Award winners' names and pictures appear in the company newspaper.

———

Federal Express has a host of awards for individual and team efforts:

✔ The Circle of Excellence Award, presented monthly to the best-performing Federal Express station, emphasizes teamwork.

✔ The Golden Falcon is awarded to employees who go "above and beyond" to serve their customers.

✔ The Bravo Zulu (Navy talk for "well done") program gives managers the prerogative of awarding a dinner, theater tickets or cash to any employee who has done an outstanding job.

✔ The Quality Achievement Award, presented annually, is the company's highest award.

———

P hil Hughes, director of human resources for Acapulco Restaurants in Long Beach, CA, reports how hourly and salaried employees are rewarded.

The company rewards its hourly employees in the following ways:

✔ $100 is awarded for hourly referrals after ninety days.

✔ $300 is awarded for management referrals after ninety days.

✔ Employee of the Month receives $50 cash, one day off and a parking space by the front door for thirty days.

✔ Bright Ideas program awards up to $1,000 for money-saving ideas that are adopted.

✔ President's Award plaque and a check for up to $2,500 for an act of outstanding service are signed and presented by the company president.

✔ Employees are treated to lunch by the department head for a job well done. Breakfast is prepared by the management staff for the line staff.

✔ Theme days throughout the year (Cinco de Mayo, Fourth of July, Halloween, Christmas) include various giveaways, trips, cash, limo rides, etc.

✔ Casual dress is allowed in the office every Friday and all week from Memorial Day to Labor Day.

> 66 What makes employees come to work is a sense of pride, recognition and achievement. Workers committed to their jobs and recognized for their work will work whatever hours it takes to get the job done. 99
>
> —THOMAS KELLEY, Chairman of the Board, Society for Human Resource Development

> **66** Provide positive, immediate, and certain consequences for people's behaviors, and they will do what you want. **99**
>
> —BARCY FOX,
> Vice President,
> Performance Systems,
> Maritz Motivation
> Company

✔ Monthly cash contests are held in the restaurants for the best server, bartender, busser, etc.

The company rewards its salaried employees as follows:

✔ Average check contest ($16,000/car Grand Prize)

✔ QSC (Quality Service Control) Monthly Award for highest score ($1,000)

✔ QSC Award for 95 percent or better ($100 each month)

✔ Safety Lotto ($500 each month; restaurant must remain accident-free that month to be eligible)

✔ General manager referral ($1,000 per referral)

✔ General Manager of the Year ($5,500 trip and one week of vacation)

✔ President's Club (plaque and recognition in company publication)

✔ President's Honor Roll (plaque and recognition in company publication)

————

Nelly Attwater, supervisor for training and development for El Torito Restaurants in Irvine, CA, reports how the restaurants use the Be a Star program. "When a manager or supervisor catches someone doing something right—or above and beyond his or her job description—that employee is given a Star Buck, which serves as a cash substitute. Each restaurant has a drawing at the end of the month for prizes (cash, TV, etc.), and each region has a drawing for prizes also ($1,000 cash, TV, VCR, etc.). Each employee can have numerous stars for the drawings."

> 66 A reward is a special gain for special achievements, a treat for doing something above-and-beyond. 99
>
> —ROSABETH MOSS KANTER, Author and Management Consultant

Nordstrom Inc., the Seattle-based department store chain, offers the Pacesetter Award to employees who have exceeded goals by a considerable margin. As a Pacesetter, an employee receives a certificate, a new business card that reads "Pacesetter" and a lavish evening of dining, dancing and entertainment to share with a guest. For the following year, the Pacesetter enjoys a 33 percent discount on all Nordstrom merchandise, 13 percent greater than the standard employee discount.

There's only one reserved parking spot at Odetics, Inc., the manufacturer of robots and spaceborne tape recorders in Anaheim, CA, and that's for the person selected as Associate of the Month.

At Ceramics Process Systems Corporation, a technical ceramics manufacturer in Milford, MA, the Extra Mile Award is given each December to several people who have gone above and beyond the call of duty. Peter Loconto, president of the company, says, "We were struggling to improve yield and productivity. One person took it upon himself to document all the issues involved and set out the problems so that management could clearly see where the obstacles were." Another person, faced with what management considered overly stringent (even unreasonable) requirements on a particular job from one customer, worked day and night—unasked—to accommodate the client's wishes. The employee got the job done on time. "When we announced the person's name, everyone in the company stood up and cheered," Loconto says. "That was a true validation of the person's hard work." Winners' names are engraved on a plaque that hangs in the company's lobby, and the chosen employees also receive either cash or equity in the company.

Denis Gagnon, senior vice president for human resources development for Meloche Monnex, an insurance banking company in Montreal, describes how outstanding performance is recognized in the company: Top performers receive a personal letter from the president, congratulating them for their achievement. They also receive an annual salary increase twice the average. A portion of the increase is paid in one lump sum when the employee's salary is high in the range. These employees also get priority in the choice of additional responsibilities and training.

Productivity/ Production/ Quality Awards

Rewards can be used specifically to encourage certain productivity, performance and production goals. According to one study, only 13 percent of the work force in this country believe they would personally benefit from producing more effectively. In a similar study in Japan, 93 percent of the workers questioned felt certain they would benefit. In addition:

✔ 89 percent of American workers think their companies would perform better if employees were given meaningful incentives to improve quality and productivity.

✔ 93 percent of workers say American products could compete better against Japanese products if American management better involved workers in continuous improvement efforts.

✔ 81 percent of workers say they would not receive any reward for an increase in productivity.

✔ 60 percent of managers believe their compensation will not increase if their performance improves.

✔ 40 percent of workers believe the average American company currently offers employees meaningful incentives to maximize quality and productivity.

People tend to be satisfied, productive and motivated when effective performance is recognized and rewarded in ways they value highly. Edward A. Kazemek, partner and national director of the Organizational Consulting Division at Laventhol & Horwath in Chicago, IL, offers insights that can help companies achieve this goal:

✔ Effective performance should be rewarded consistently. When the employee experiences no reward or inconsistent rewards, performance may drop because the employee sees high performance as a dead end.

✔ Poor performance should not be automatically rewarded. Across-the-board cost of living adjustments and seniority increases often result in financial rewards unrelated to performance.

✔ Doing what one finds rewarding should result in effective performance.

✔ Management should take the time to find out about the needs and desires of those reporting to them.

In almost any performance improvement program, rewards and recognition are integral to the program's success.

Bob Vassallo, manager of employee relations at the Thomas J. Lipton Company, maker of food products in Englewood Cliffs, NJ, reports having an Open Vending Machine Day in which employees are allowed free access to plant cafeteria vending machines for reaching certain manufacturing goals, such as productivity, quality and safety.

At Collins & Aikman, a carpet manufacturer based in Dalton, GA, a rewards and recognition committee proposes and evaluates rewards for a wide range of employee achievements such as performance, cost improvement and safety.

———

Motorola in Schaumburg, IL, has awards breakfasts at which factory workers who have met certain quality goals are recognized by senior managers. Managers are empowered to award dinner for two at a four-star restaurant or a weekend at a first-class hotel for doing a good job on a project.

———

If production meets certain specified goals, employees are given an additional week of paid vacation between Christmas and New Year's at Marion Laboratories in Kansas City, MO, in a program called Uncommon Winter.

———

James Allchin, head software guru at the Microsoft Corporation in Redmond, WA, rewarded programmers for meeting a key milestone on a project code-named "Cairo" by finding a camel and bringing it into the office. The camel was an immediate hit with the Cairo team, who petted it and had their pictures taken with it.

———

66 Offering incentives is the most positive way to reward achievement goals, improve service and develop cost-saving programs. **99**

—Advertisement for
Thomson Consumer
Electronic, Inc.

> 66 We ask a driver to set his own goal. Say he sets it at eighteen hundred pounds per hour. If he falls below it, we'll sit down and disscuss why. We may decide to reduce it somewhat and try to reach the lower goal. If he goes higher than eighteen hundred, we'll make sure to give him some kind of recognition, if it is only by telling him what a great job he's doing. 99
>
> —TOM ENGLISH,
> Terminal Manager,
> Preston Trucking

A CASE STUDY IN IMPROVED PERFORMANCE

When Lou Gerstner became president of Travel Related Services (TRS) at New York-based American Express, the unit was facing one of its biggest challenges in AMEX's 130-year history. Hundreds of banks were offering or planning to introduce credit cards through Visa and MasterCard that would compete with the American Express card. And more than two dozen financial service firms were coming into the traveler's checks business.

Within a week of his appointment, Gerstner brought together the people running the card organization and questioned all the principles by which they conducted their business. In particular, he challenged two widely shared beliefs— that the division should have only one product, the green card, and that this product was limited in potential for growth and innovation.

Gerstner also moved quickly to develop a more entrepreneurial culture, to hire and train people who would thrive in it, and to communicate to them clearly the overall direction. He and other top managers rewarded intelligent risk-taking. To make entrepreneurship easier, they discouraged unnecessary bureaucracy. They also upgraded hiring standards and created the TRS Graduate Management program, which offered high-potential young people special training, an enriched set of experiences and an unusual degree of exposure to people in top management. To encourage risk-taking among all TRS employees, Gerstner established a Great Performers program (similar to the program at Honeywell described earlier) to recognize and reward truly exceptional customer service, a central tenet of the organization's philosophy.

In the Great Performers program, life-sized posters showing famous people with their greatest performances were displayed throughout the facilities for many weeks. Then the company began to picture American Express employees on posters, with a statement of a major accomplishment by each employee. Afterwards the employee could take the poster home.

Nominations were made by fellow employees, supervisors and customers. Award winners were eligible to become Grand Award winners, named by the worldwide governing committee. There was no limit on how many people could win, and in a recent year thirty-eight employees captured the award. Prizes for Grand Award winners included an all-expense-paid trip for two to New York, $4,000 in American Express traveler's checks, a platinum "GP" logo pin and a framed certificate.

These initiatives led quickly to new markets, products and services and resulted in an increase in TRS's net income of 500 percent in eleven years, or about an 18 percent annual compounded rate. With a return on equity of 28 percent, the business outperformed many so-called high-tech, high-growth companies, as well as most low-growth but high-profit businesses.

> ❝ We all like to be recognized and appreciated. Just by giving an award or recognition certificate, formally recognizing someone in front of a group or even buying a cup of coffee, we're telling the employees that their work is appreciated. ❞
>
> —HARVEY STEIN,
> President,
> Stein & Read Incentives

> **❝ Incentives offer that extra 'thank you' for sustaining high performance. ❞**
>
> —CHARLES GEHL,
> Coordinator,
> Frank Implement Company

The Outstanding Teller Service Award at the First-Knox National Bank in Mt. Vernon, OH, seeks to tie productivity and customer service awards to measurable goals. The program selects one outstanding teller from each branch based on the following system: 33 percent teller choice, 34 percent customer satisfaction (based on selection cards in customers' bank statements), 11 percent balancing record, 11 percent number of transactions and 11 percent supervisory rating.

The Ring of Quality program was established at ITT in New York to recognize people who had offered outstanding support to the quality program for a period of five years, or had accomplished one sensational, specific and unique act. It quickly became a peer recognition program. Hundreds of gold rings have been presented to winners, as have hundreds of silver pins and other citations. Employees take the program very seriously. The corporate president or chairman presents the awards at a formal dinner. Based on the reactions to the rings and pins, one thing is very clear: Cash or financial awards are not personal enough to provide effective recognition.

At Martin Marietta Aggregates in Raleigh, NC, Ray Merritt, training manager, provides M&M's candy, doughnuts or gourmet coffee as one way to recognize "above and beyond" performance or to celebrate the achievement of a specific goal. An extra vacation day is also awarded for outstanding performance such as achievement of goals or exceptional customer service.

———

F aced with employee morale problems resulting from rapid growth, Ridgeway Development Corporation in Atlanta implemented a promotion among its workers by mailing a giant card to their homes each month. The first card contained a mirror and the words, "Face it . . . you make the difference." Next a small calendar arrived, along with an invitation to participate in the employee suggestion program and a ballot for the Employee of the Month, Go the Extra Mile Award. Later mailings included an expandable sponge labeled "Expand your product knowledge and we'll both grow" and a nightlight bearing an energy-conservation message. The promotion lasted six months and produced eighty-two Extra-Mile nominations. Productivity also increased 25 percent.

———

> 66 There is no way a work force that is uninvolved and unrewarded will be quality-conscious, efficient or innovative. 99
>
> —AARON SUGARMAN,
> *Incentive*

Employee Suggestion Awards

O nly 41 percent of surveyed employees believe the average company listens to employees' ideas. The average American worker makes only one or two suggestions per year; the average Japanese worker, however, submits hundreds of suggestions to his or her employer annually. Most companies have some type of employee suggestion program; here is how some of the more innovative companies reward employee suggestions.

> 66 Companies have to reward people for being creative, for coming up with new ideas. 99
>
> —TOM PETERS,
> Author and
> Management Consultant

O ne Amoco plant in Texas City, TX, uses a suggestion plan that has saved Amoco $18.8 million in two years. The plant awards winning suggesters gift certificates in front of their fellow workers during lunch breaks, publicizing them on the refinery's internal TV system and in local newspapers and entering them in contests for Employee of the Month or Year. Winners garner gifts like pen-and-pencil sets and week-long vacations, which are presented by the plant manager at plant-wide dinners.

A t Garrett Resources Group, a management training and consulting firm in Albuquerque, NM, front-line employees are asked for ways to save money, according to CEO Milt Garrett.

They put their responses on three- by five-inch cards and are paid $3 cash for each idea. If the idea is implemented, they are paid an additional $25 in cash or 10 percent of the savings, whichever is greater.

———

The Championship Way program at General Mills, headquartered in Minneapolis, includes a general session followed by meetings of small groups of employees to examine their work environments and make recommendations for improvements. The program is designed to reinforce company values and includes a reward system that closely ties pay to performance.

———

Urban Bianchi, a machinist with Cleveland-based Parker Hannifin Corporation, has turned in more than 800 cost-cutting proposals that his bosses have approved—so many that the *Los Angeles Times* has dubbed him "the undisputed king of the suggestion box." The company has rewarded him with a flood of microwave ovens, coupons for free dinners, tools, and other gifts, with an estimated value of $17,000 in a four-year period. "I've got so much stuff, it's unbelievable," Bianchi says. While he adds that for him doing a job well is what's motivating, he also admits that he gets a kick out of sharing his riches with family members. "When I gave them radios, they loved it," he says. "It meant more to them that I got [a radio] doing a good job, working hard, than if I'd bought it at a store."

———

> ❝ There's nothing wrong with a cash award, but then it's spent. Seemingly small gestures— a parking spot, a plaque, bulletin boards with pictures of employees—can be as effective as banquets and travel. ❞
>
> —DONALD GAGNON, Training Coordinator, Brunswick Mining and Smelting Corp. (Gagnon was named Suggester of the Year by the National Association of Suggestion Systems.)

☛ *When an employee presents an idea or suggestion, thank the person for his or her concern and initiative.*

Arthur Hogling, executive director of the Jefferson County Community Center in Lakewood, CO, reports, "In our corporate culture, 'playing hardball' means being aggressive in saving our organization money by finding cost-saving methods or diligently pursuing new sources of revenue. Employees demonstrating this skill receive a baseball at our monthly meetings. The balls are signed by our management team and have become a source of pride on employees' desks."

John Deere Dubuque Tractor Works in Dubuque, IA, doubled employee participation in an employee suggestion program by providing all participants with pocket protectors, magnetic calendars and notepads imprinted with the slogan "Got an idea? Write it down!" Employees whose suggestions were implemented received additional awards in a personal presentation.

Grumman Corporation, the aerospace firm headquartered in Bethpage, NY, was able to respond more quickly to employee suggestions once it began using gift certificates. "There's more of a sense of immediacy with gift certificates," says Marilyn Lage, senior buyer in the procurement department. "We needed to award something tangible, but quickly. With 26,100 employees nationwide, the [previous] program had become very unwieldy." Now supervisors keep the gift certificates in their desk drawers and dispense them within a day if an employee's suggestion is implemented.

———

In three months, the American Achievers program at American Airlines inspired nearly 3,500 seven-person teams to come up with more than 1,600 ideas that were adopted, resulting in more than $20 million in cost-saving or revenue-generating improvements. Employees reaped $4.7 million in merchandise prizes, with each prize based on the cash value of the idea implemented. More importantly, the employees wholeheartedly supported the changes because they had designed them. That success has led to a continuing system called AAchievers that includes instant points-for-merchandise rewards for good work by individuals and groups.

The American Achievers program seeks to recognize employees for anything special they do, or simply for consistently doing a good job. Managers, crew chiefs, lead agents and other supervisors can award Achiever points at any time to any employee. For example, points can be awarded for perfect attendance throughout a bad winter or can be awarded on the spot to a worker for helping a passenger with an emergency. The points are issued on certificates that can be cashed in for travel benefits or for merchandise from a catalog compiled for the program.

———

Warner-Lambert, the pharmaceutical company based in Morris Plains, NJ, uses gift certificates for an on-the-spot employee recogni-

> 66 There's nothing more important than making certain that each employee feels respected and valued. 99
>
> —ROBERT CRANDALL, CEO, American Airlines

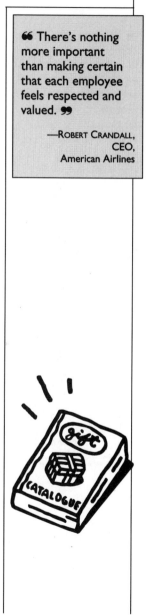

tion program that was recently introduced. "We wanted to acknowledge our employees' suggestions and ideas right then and there," says Katherine King, manager of administrative policy.

Participants in one of Action Management Associates' problem-solving and decision-making workshops were given a certificate commemorating their achievement when they used techniques they had learned in a training program. The implemented programs resulted in a minimum of $20,000 in documented improvements, cost reduction or gross profit. Trainers whose combined graduates had saved more than $1 million were named to the Million Dollar Club.

The pharmaceuticals company Cyanamid Canada's Key to Innovation campaign encouraged workers to contribute ideas and become Frequent Innovators. For productivity-enhancing ideas, employees received from 40 to 1,000 points, redeemable in an award catalog for such prizes as glassware, radios, televisions and weekend trips for two.

Everyone Counts is a program at Black & Decker, headquartered in Towson, MD, that uses teams to brainstorm and develop ideas about training, communication, administration and rewards. People from different departments were grouped into thirty-nine teams, and two evaluation committees for managerial personnel were named to receive ideas and judge their merit. The evaluation teams also noted leadership potential in some employees when they made their presentations. A total of two hundred ideas were submitted and fifty-nine approved. The twelve ideas that have already been implemented have dealt mostly with improved operations that resulted in cost savings. One $700,000 idea concerned the substitution of a new material in one of the company's product lines. The program also improved the upward lines of communication in the company.

> **❝** We believe that most people have capabilities beyond those they are called on to demonstrate in their jobs. **❞**
>
> —From a statement of philosophy printed by Hewitt Associates

---

At Eastman Kodak in Rochester, NY, an employee whose suggestion is implemented receives 15 percent of the out-of-pocket savings achieved in the first two years of use. If a suggestion results in a new product, the award is equal to 3 percent of the sales achieved in the first year. Kodak has given awards—averaging $3 million annually—to more than 30,000 people.

Fel-Pro, a gasket manufacturer based in Skokie, IL, once a year holds a drawing for $1,000 for all employees who participated in the firm's suggestion program.

At Levi Strauss & Company, based in San Francisco, employees nominate one another for the firm's Koshland Award for showing initiative, taking risks, generating cost-saving

> **❝** Our early emphasis on human relations was not motivated by altruism, but by the simple belief that if we respected our people and helped them respect themselves the company would make the most profit. **❞**
>
> —THOMAS J. WATSON, JR.,
> Former CEO,
> IBM

measures, coming up with creative ideas for promoting products at the retail level—anything that puts the company at a competitive advantage. Winners receive a plaque at an annual awards ceremony and a cash prize.

A CASE STUDY IN RECOGNIZING EMPLOYEE SUGGESTIONS

IBM's suggestion program awards $50 to $150,000 for money-saving ideas or suggestions with intangible benefits like enhanced health, safety or customer service. The amount of the award for an idea that leads to a measurable savings is based on 25 percent of the first year's net material and labor savings. For awards of more than $200, the suggester also receives 25 percent of projected net savings for the second year, up to $150,000.

Awards for suggestions that yield intangible benefits depend on such factors as the seriousness of the problem, creativity and the effectiveness of the solution. These awards usually range from $50 to $100, although the $150,000 maximum applies here as well. The program is open to all employees. In a recent year IBM gave out eight $150,000 awards, out of 153,000 ideas submitted by its 223,000 U.S. employees. Other award programs include:

Invention Achievement Award Plan. These awards recognize a significant record of invention. The first patent application the employee files under the provisions of the plan earns

$1,500. Employees receive points for patent applications and other qualifying inventions that are published. At each twelve-point plateau, the employee gets a certificate and $3,600. The first plateau also earns jewelry.

IBM Division Award Plan. This award recognizes and rewards achievements that have "outstanding value" to the company in terms of cost savings and the impact on the major mission of a specific division. Awards range from $1,500 to $25,000.

Informal Award Plan. Many IBM operating units and locations provide Dinner for Two or Night on the Town awards to employees for extraordinary efforts that help achieve a particular goal.

———

A t the 10,000-person Honda of America factory in Marysville, OH, employees receive $100 for each accepted suggestion, but they also get anywhere from 1 to 12 VIP points for each one. If they make a presentation to a quality circle meeting, they get an extra 50 points. When they accumulate 300 points, they get a plaque; 1,000 points nets $800. Higher-level prizes are a Honda Civic for 2,500 points, and an Accord, two extra weeks of vacation and four weeks' pay for 5,000 points. The company received more than 10,000 suggestions in a recent year, resulting in savings of $5 million.

———

> 66 If managers ask people to give of their creative talents and commitment and to take apparent risks by doing such things as proposing labor-saving ideas, those people should share handsomely in any profit that results. 99
>
> —TOM PETERS,
> Author and
> Management Consultant

Ewing Kauffman, chairman and founder of Marion Laboratories in Kansas City, MO, handed out $7,000, $12,000 and $15,000 worth of company stock to three employees for money-saving suggestions. Some 10,000 shares of stock are distributed annually among those with the best suggestions. One year resulted in an average of $1,000 worth of stock apiece for the employees whose 237 suggestions were accepted.

Customer Service Awards

S atisfying customers is a goal most companies want to reinforce and constantly recognize. It costs five times more, some estimates have it, to win a new customer than to keep an existing one. Here are reinforcers that companies have used to help encourage customer service.

A t Hecht's hardware stores, based in Arlington, VA, employees win points toward a shopping spree if managers hear them calling customers by name.

———

L ensCrafters optical stores, headquartered in Cincinnati, granted $100 bonus checks for outstanding customer service, with the top nine people getting $1,000 and a crystal memento.

———

I n Todays Way Giveaway at Dallas-based Todays Temporary, every time a temporary employee exceeds a client's expectations, he or she is entered in an annual drawing for prizes. Clients rate temporary employees on evaluation cards, which are then submitted to the company. Approximately 950 prizes have been awarded to employees over three years.

———

> 66 Any time you make people feel better about themselves, you are building strong motivation. 99
>
> —REBECCA BOYLE,
> Manager,
> Training Services,
> Empire of America
> Federal Savings Bank

PLAY THE NAME GAME

☛ *Whenever a service employee thanks a customer by name, have the customer drop a coupon with the employee's name into a big box. Give the employees who have thanked the most customers by name a cash reward.*

"Recognizing people, making them feel special, is a great way to boost morale and quality at the same time," says Mitch Rosenberg, director of human resources, planning and development for American Savings Bank, headquartered in Irvine, CA. "You can see the difference." That was the idea behind the Service Pride Award, given to employees who were "caught in the act" of delivering exceptional service. Peers, managers and supervisors nominate individuals. The applications are judged by a panel of seven employees, rotated yearly, ranging from mail clerk to supervisor. One winner per month receives a lapel pin and a congratulatory letter, presented by the supervisor in front of peers. Each winner then becomes eligible for a quarterly award for the best service act. From the quarterly award winners, judges select an annual winner, who is flown to Irvine, housed in a luxurious hotel, chauffeured via limousine to a posh restaurant to dine with ASB executives, and presented with the Service Pride Award.

McDonald's contracted with Lenox Awards to make available to its owner/operators jewelry bearing the company's well-known "golden arches" logo. These are distributed to employees who provide superior service.

Every month at the Nordstrom department store chain, based in Seattle, each store's managers meet to pick a Customer Service All-Star—the person who has made the most striking service contribution for that period. Managers draw from their own observations, customer comment sheets placed near every cash register, reports by "mystery shoppers" and letters from customers. The winner gets $100, "Customer Service All-Star" stamped on his or her business card, and a larger employee discount on store merchandise. A Customer Service All-Star store is also picked each month, with headquarters providing prize money for a storewide barbecue or pizza party.

The Omni Service Champions program of Omni Hotels recognizes employees who go out of their way to deliver extraordinary service to customers with medals, ribbon pins for their uniforms, cash, dinner, recognition in the company's newspaper and on posters in each hotel and, finally, a three-day celebration at an Omni hotel chosen by company executives. At the end of the year, the three employees from each hotel who received the most commendations are awarded medals (gold, silver and bronze) and cash prizes ($1,000 for gold, and $500 each for silver and bronze), and all attend a gala.

Louise Boyd, director of education for Episcopal Retirement Homes, headquartered in Cincinnati, reports a program called Applause Pause, in which any employee can drop an index card with an anecdote about outstanding internal or external customer service into a box. The boxes are opened weekly and each card is given

> 66 Fancy sales pitches, high-powered marketing strategies and clever advertising can be very important attention-getters. And they may persuade people to become your customer. But keeping customers for any period of time depends on how well you reward them. 99
>
> —MICHAEL LEBOEUF, *How to Win Customers and Keep Them for Life*

☞ *Award a silver pin or similar prize for reported positive customer comments.*

to the employee's supervisor, who passes it on to the employee.

———

In New Jersey Transit's Customer Service Awards program, employees who serve the public directly earn awards for exemplary customer service, while internal workers such as secretaries, maintenance people and accountants receive awards for service to other employees. Two months before the awards are announced at the end of each year, posters with ballots are placed in train stations and at bus stops. Both riders and employees can make nominations for the awards, as can vendors who sell supplies to the agency.

In a recent year, the agency received 300 nominations and chose 10 winners, according to spokesperson Sandra Check. The number of ballots a person receives is taken into account, but the quality of the nomination is more important. "If we have one nomination for a person, but it's outstanding, that person might win." A nominating committee made up of managers selects the winners. Among the criteria they use are exceptional customer service, especially to correct something that has gone wrong; demonstrated creativity or resourcefulness in assisting a customer; and development of new ways to solve problems.

The type of award varies each year. Past winners received savings bonds and a two-day trip to Atlantic City, and each recipient also gets a plaque or trophy. Awards are given out at an annual company-wide meeting held at a conference center.

> 66 Empowerment is the recognition that employees are not as dumb as employers thought they were. 99
>
> —Darryl Hartley-Leonard, President, Hyatt Hotels Corp.

"We are a customer-driven company," Check says, "and we thought this would be a good way to recognize the assets of our employees. They look forward to seeing who gets recognized for their work."

———

The Good Samaritan Hospital in Cincinnati instituted a recognition and reward program to improve customer service that incorporates monthly drawings and internal publicity, but also uses continuing training to reinforce a list of ten performance standards on which the program is based. To make sure goals, criteria and progress are being communicated constantly, all 3,200 employees attend a one-hour training session every other month.

———

Delta Airlines has a Feather in Your Cap Award for customer service above and beyond the call of duty, such as that provided by the flight attendant who drove a passenger from Houston to Beaumont, Texas, for a funeral she would otherwise have been unable to attend because she missed her connecting flight.

———

At The Andersons Management Corporation retail stores in Maumee, OH, store managers were given a certain number of silver dollars to give out when they observed good customer service or received comments from customers or employees about employees who provided noteworthy service, reports Mike

> 66 People want to feel empowered to find better ways to do things and to take responsibility for their own environment. Allowing them to do this has had a big impact on how they do their jobs, as well as on their satisfaction with the company. 99
>
> —JAMES BERDAHL, Vice President of Marketing, Business Incentives

> ❝ People who feel appreciated by their employers identify with the organization and are more willing to give their best to the job. ❞
>
> —PEGGY STUART, Assistant Editor, *Personnel Journal*

McCartney, human resource development internal consultant. Employees who received silver dollars were enrolled in the Silver Dollar Club and became eligible for monthly prize drawings.

A t First Union Banks in Charlotte, NC, "secret shoppers" are used to award $200 on the spot to lending officers who follow a scripted procedure with customers: stand up, smile, shake hands and so on.

A t FMC Lithium Division (a subsidiary of FMC Corporation) in Bessemer City, NC, managers take deserving employees on trips to visit customers or certain vendors, reports Wayne Gray, Area II production superintendent. The involvement not only recognizes those operators for their good efforts, but it also helps educate them and builds a sense of ownership of their jobs and the company's products. FMC found that the additional cost is more than repaid in increased motivation and overall business understanding.

C ontinental Airlines mailed Pride in Performance certificates to its top 50,000 frequent fliers and asked them to pass the certificates out to particularly helpful employees. Continental workers could redeem the certificates for dinners, luggage, hotel stays, flight passes and other merchandise.

J. W. Wade, superintendent at Shenandoah National Park in Luray, VA, reports that employees developed an Excellence in Service Award, which they administer. It is designed to recognize those on the park staff, as well as outside cooperators, who make significant contributions to the mission and purposes of the park. The award consists of a letter and a certificate with artwork done by a ranger artist.

> 66 Good treatment of workers results in similar treatment of customers. 99
>
> —TODD ENGLANDER,
> *Incentive*

In its Service Excellence Award, Citibank in New York rewards employees at any level except senior management who demonstrate what is deemed to be outstanding customer service. An employee is nominated by his or her manager; then the nominee is reviewed by the various levels of management within the employee's division. Award winners usually get a gift certificate for up to $500 in merchandise.

Denny's restaurant chain, based in Spartanburg, SC, sought to recognize employees and customer service by creating the Personal Best recognition program. Each employee was given a ribbon bearing the words "For you, the guest, my personal best" to wear at work. Employees voted each month for the recipient in their job area who best personified customer service. Lapel pins were awarded indicating the number of months the employee had won the award.

The Eagle Award is used at SKF Bearing Industries Company in King of Prussia, PA. Each employee is given two Eagle Award coins to give to other employees for outstanding customer service along with a certificate briefly describing the service received. Employees who receive five or more Eagle Awards are given a decorative display holder. Employees have the option to exchange ten Eagle Awards for a $50 American Express Be My Guest gift certificate. Recipients are recognized on bulletin boards in all facilities, and some of the more noteworthy examples are highlighted in "Quest for Quality," a company newsletter. The employee who receives the most Eagle Awards in a six-month period is recognized with a trophy and a $250 American Express gift certificate at the president's semi-annual State of the Company meeting. Jeff Minkoff, corporate quality assurance manager, reports that more than 1,500 Eagle Awards were given out in the first one and a half years of the program.

> 66 Knowing that what you do is important and appreciated is the best reward. 99
>
> —JOHN BALL,
> Service Training Manager,
> American Honda
> Motor Company

The President's Award of the Los Angeles-based Executive Life Insurance Company is designed to recognize individuals who make an extra effort in service. "Since Executive Life is a service company, we must always give our customers the best service possible," says Kenneth R. Wilson, manager of employee benefits. "The better the service, the fewer the problems and thus the higher the productivity." The award—a fourteen-karat gold apple tie tack—is given to individuals who earn the EEE (Extra Executive Effort) Award.

———

Minneapolis-based AmeriData Systems provides an incentive called Partner of the Quarter to maintain a caring attitude toward customers and coworkers. "We believe all employees, from the janitor to the president, are partners in the success or failure of the company," says Sharon Berglund, personnel director. "Everyone has a role to play in the ultimate goal of excellent customer satisfaction."

———

The Service Leader Award program at the American Hospital Association in Chicago offers winners a $100 check, a certificate and an engraved plaque at the monthly manager's meeting. A Service Leader of the Year is selected from the twelve monthly leaders. That person receives a $100 check and an engraved plaque.

———

In the Most Valuable Player program at St. Louis's Busch Stadium, ten randomly selected fans are given two small MVP cards, which they can bestow on any two employees who show them some courtesy—defined as "a smile, a welcome, a way of handling a question or problem," according to Vicki Hutchison, manager of special projects for the Civic Center Corporation. Employees then turn the cards over to supervisors; if the group of workers collects at least fif-

> 66 If you're going to strive to motivate workers through autonomy and empowerment, it's important to remember that the primary burden is to make sure employees believe what you say. Don't tell them you want them to be empowered to increase the company's profits. Tell them you want them to be empowered because it's the best way to remain competitive and guarantee everyone their jobs. 99
>
> —CARL ROBINSON,
> Vice-President,
> Organizational Psychologists

> **❝ Compensation is a right; recognition is a gift. ❞**
>
> —ROSABETH MOSS KANTER,
> Author and
> Management Consultant

teen of the twenty cards during the game, a drawing is held and the winner gets a $100 bill. All employees who receive cards from fans are mentioned in a monthly flyer sent out to employees.

A monthly Outstanding Teamworker program encourages workers to nominate fellow All-Stars, who receive recognition in the form of a pregame on-the-field ceremony, a lapel pin, their choice of merchandise from a catalog and brunch in their honor.

———

At the Inter-Continental Hilton Head hotel in South Carolina, an Employee of the Month is selected based on guest questionnaires that evaluate service, with some comments by managers. Those honored receive cash, a plaque, a preferred parking space, lunch with the general manager and a stay in a suite with complimentary meals and beverages.

———

At Park Lane Hotels International, based in San Francisco, guests are asked to nominate hotel workers who provided outstanding service. The company rewarded all nominees with Sony Watchman TVs and held a grand-prize drawing for a twenty-inch TV; the guest who nominated the grand-prize winner received two free nights at the hotel.

———

MCI Communications Corporation, based in Washington, DC, used picnic baskets from Harry and David in Medford, OR, to reward fifty of its customer-service reps. "MCI wanted to recognize employees who saw a problem and stepped right in to solve it," says Jon Silver, a sales rep for Harry and David. A note of appreciation was tucked inside each basket.

———

Indianapolis-based Cellular One has a bonus plan that awards car phone installers $10 for every customer compliment they get (mostly on customer comments cards) and deducts $10 every time a customer complains about an installation and $20 if a customer's vehicle is damaged during an installation. Vehicle damage has fallen by 70 percent, and customer compliments have tripled since the company began operation.

———

The San Diego Convention and Visitors Bureau awards the title Cab Driver of the Year to the driver who exemplifies outstanding hospitality toward both visitors and residents. The winner is feted at the city's Annual Cab Driver Appreciation Day, and receives 500 business cards, an engraved dashboard plaque and a magnetic sign for the cab that announces the award. One recent winner, Montag Plank, says he provides riders with extras such as newspapers and information about local attractions. "No matter what your job is, if you're courteous and do the job right, people will respect you for it," he says.

———

> **"** We will move mountains to let our employees and customers know we care. I've traveled 4,000 miles to spend five minutes with a customer, to let her know how important her business is to us. Caring is contagious, and we try to spread it around. **"**
>
> —HARVEY MACKAY,
> President,
> Mackay Envelope Corp.

> 66 One of the step-
> ping stones to a
> world-class operation
> is to tap into the cre-
> ative and intellectual
> power of each and
> every employee. 99
>
> —HAROLD A. POLING,
> Chairman and CEO,
> Ford Motor Company

When Dick Radell, vice president of human resources for Marcus Restaurants in Milwaukee, receives exceptional service at one of the company's restaurants, he writes a short note on the back of his business card and gives it to the server immediately.

Joan Cawley, director of human resources for Advanta Corporation, the financial services firm in Horsham, PA, describes a monthly recognition program called the GEM (Going the Extra Mile) Award for customer-service representatives. Each month peers and managers select an employee whose specific performances went beyond the call of duty for a customer. Each winner's name is added to an engraved brass plaque, and he or she enjoys a rotating crystal desktop plaque for the month. Photos are taken at the award presentation (held at a staff meeting) and made into a colorful collage that decorates the department wall. At the end of each program year, the names of the twelve winners are put into a hat for a prize drawing. The grand prize is a cruise for two.

A CASE STUDY IN CUSTOMER SERVICE

66 We share the dream to be recognized as the very best company when it comes to delivering value to customers, employees, shareholders and communities," says Kent B.

Foster, president of GTE Telephone Operations, headquartered in Stamford, CT. To help reach that dream, the President's Quality Awards program offers awards to employees in four categories: area and region, individual employees, teams, and vendors.

The company's four areas and fourteen regions compete each year for Quality Champion Cups. Award recipients are selected directly by customers who are surveyed annually. The most improved region is also recognized with a trophy.

Individual employees are recognized at three levels of achievement: The top ten employees receive $2,500 along with a personalized award and a letter of commendation from the division president. The thirty finalists receive $750 and a personalized award, and the forty semifinalists receive $500 and a personalized award. One individual who has demonstrated exemplary commitment to quality is chosen for the Individual Quality Champions to receive the President's Distinctive Commendation. He or she receives a monetary award, a special medallion and a letter of commendation from the president.

Team awards are given to two first-place Gold Award winners (one for external and one for internal customer service), two second-place Silver Award winners and three Bronze Award winners for external efforts. Members of each team receive cash, a personalized award and a letter of commendation from the president.

In 1987, GTE started recognizing its major suppliers who represented the highest standards in its Partners in Quality program.

> 66 It's vital that you motivate your people—customers and employees—anyone who can contribute to the company's success. 99
>
> —ROBERT EVANS,
> Director,
> Promotional Services,
> Gillette Company

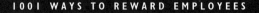

> 66 From the begin-
> ning I was empow-
> ered to take
> responsibility to deal
> with clients directly.
> It adds a lot of satis-
> faction to the job
> and, compared to
> what my peers tell
> me about their work,
> this is an oasis. 99
>
> —IAN HARRIS,
> Actuarial Consultant,
> Hewitt Associates

Nominations for the President's Quality Awards come from customers, peers, management, or in the case of the regional awards, through customer survey data. After a local review, top nominees are forwarded to the national headquarters executive committee for the final selections.

All award winners, their guests and selected employees from each area and headquarters are brought to Dallas for a grand reception and dinner hosted by senior executives. The following afternoon, nominees, their guests and selected employees host an Academy Awards-type ceremony at the Morton H. Meyerson Symphony Center in downtown Dallas. After the awards ceremony comes a lavish theme party honoring the winners.

Sales Goal Awards

One of the more easily quantifiable achievements in most companies is the attainment of sales goals. For that reason, sales reinforcers are fairly commonplace in most for-profit organizations.

Paul Levine, general manager of Miller Nissan in Van Nuys, CA, awards $5 to the first salesperson who sells a car on a given day—then gives that person $5 for every other car sold by any salesperson on the lot that day. Levine awards $5 to the salesperson who sells the second car on a given day—and gives that person $5 for every car sold thereafter on that day . . . and so on. The first person to make a sale can win $100 in a day just for selling one car, and as much as $200 or $300 if he or she sells more cars.

> **66** All in all, recognizing successful salespeople may be the single most critical way to boost sales results. **99**
>
> —Nancy Grden-Ellson, Senior Vice President, Market Development, Citizens and Southern National Bank of South Carolina

At Coronet/MTI Film and Video in Deerfield, IL, Mary Jo Scarpelli, sales director, brings the sales team bagels and cream cheese on the last Friday of each month.

Blanchard Training and Development in Escondido, CA, hosted an ice-cream social to celebrate a record sales month.

> **❝** If you're going to help people reach their potential, they need to be recognized and rewarded. Everyone needs that. **❞**
>
> —JACQUELINE NORCEL,
> Principal,
> Tashua Elementary School

Richard Meyerson, president of Traveltrust Corporation in San Diego, offered to remodel a nursery in a sales manager's home to accommodate a newborn child if the manager made her sales goals. She met her goals. While the remodeling was being completed, she lived in a house owned by the corporation. On another occasion, the company rewarded a male employee with a fully paid paternity leave.

———

At Chicago-based CompuMat, one of the fastest-growing computer retailers in the country, employees are rewarded for their sales numbers, and these rewards can be doubled or tripled if they also meet planning and customer relations objectives tailored for each individual.

———

❝I try to put myself in their place," says Jennifer Hurwitz, who designs incentive programs for employees of LensCrafters, the one-hour eyewear stores based in Cincinnati. "I remember my retail store experience of working hard for thirteen hours a day on my feet, and I try to design something that will make it a new and interesting day for our people each time they come to work." For example, newly opened stores with expectations of more than $100,000 in sales during their grand opening week are targeted for special attention to help them reach that goal. The whole company is on alert to watch the daily figures as they are transmitted to every location by computer. On the final day, if the store is nearing its goal, says Hurwitz, "the president and key people from the home office are flown in on a company plane for the last few hours to cheer them on and help them out, and then everyone is taken out for dinner and a big party, with awards given out right then to every person who contributes."

M ary Kay Cosmetics awards pink Cadillacs, mink coats and diamond rings to leading independent sellers.

A dvanced Micro Devices, a manufacturer and marketer of complex monolithic circuits in Sunnyvale, CA, launched an American Dream sales campaign as an incentive for reaching $200 million in sales. The reward was nothing less than a house. Every employee's name went into a hat for a drawing in case the goal was reached. Jerry Sanders, president and founder, had local reporters accompany him on his unannounced visit to the home of the winner, Jocelyn Lleno, an AMD factory line worker. Lleno was handed a check for $1,000 and was to receive the same amount every month for the next twenty years to buy her house. Two other employees received Cadillac Sevilles.

A spectacular method for recognizing and motivating outstanding employees was created for Pitney Bowes, based in Stamford, CT, by Multi Image Productions, Inc. of San Diego, which produces shows incorporating slides, film,

> **❝** Recognition is something a manager should be doing all the time—it's a running dialogue with people. **❞**
>
> —RON ZEMKE,
> Senior Editor,
> *Training*

> **66** I try to remember that people—good, intelligent, capable people—may actually need day-to-day praise and thanks for the job they do. I try to remember to get up out of my chair, turn off my computer, go sit or stand next to them and see what they're doing, ask about the challenges, find out if they need additional help, offer that help if possible, and most of all, tell them in all honesty that what they are doing is important: to me, to the company and to our customers. **99**
>
> —JOHN BALL,
> Service Training Manager,
> American Honda Motor
> Company

video, music, dancing and spectacular lighting displays. Pitney Bowes' top sales producers were recognized during the show produced and staged in Kona, Hawaii. "Our goal was to give them a type of business theater in which they would feel entertained as well as motivated to reach their goals for next year," says Multi Image Productions president and CEO Fredric W. Ashman. Budgets for these productions range from $10,000 to $1.5 million.

The life insurance industry uses an elite club, the Million Dollar Roundtable, to recognize and give status and special privileges to top salespeople.

Every employee in the New York and Hollywood offices of the Leo Burnett Company was flown first-class to the advertising agency's Chicago headquarters for the annual breakfast celebration when the company first reached $1 billion in advertising revenues.

Hewlett-Packard marketers send pistachio nuts to salespeople who excel or who close an important sale.

In a speech at a holiday party, Alan Ashton, president of WordPerfect Corporation, told the company that if it doubled its sales in the upcoming year, all 600 employees and their spouses would be invited to take a week's expense-paid vacation in Hawaii. The software developer and distributor based in Orem, UT, achieved that goal and sent employees, ten at a time, on their vacations over an eight-month period.

————

When Levi Strauss & Co., headquartered in San Francisco, reached $1 billion in sales in 1975, its executives gave out more than $2 million worth of stock and cash to employees as rewards. When it passed the $2 billion level in 1979, employees once again received significant cash awards.

————

"Peer pressure can be used constructively in many ways—employee by employee, branch by branch, or region by region," reports Nancy Grden-Ellson, senior vice president of market development at Citizens and Southern National Bank of South Carolina. "While the reports themselves can serve as a measure of performance, there is nothing like a specially created newsletter or column in the employee newspaper that discusses, in a friendly way, the battles among the sales forces. Wagers and inexpensive gifts can be used to escalate the efforts—for example, items with the corporate logo or a roving plaque for the best branch." Stories in the employee newsletter highlighting a salesperson (or branch or department) have a double effect in that the individual is recognized and a role model is created. That individual can also provide sales tips—without the formality of a training program.

———

If an operator of Chick-Fil-A, an Atlanta-based restaurant chain, increases sales by 40 percent over the previous year's sales, he or she earns the right to drive a Mark VII Lincoln Continental for one year. If the increase is repeated the following year, the operator gets the car for good. More than 100 operators have won Continentals.

———

Security systems manufacturer Checkpoint Systems in Thorofare, NJ, names its top eight salespeople to its President's Club. Club members act as an advisory council to the company's top executives and get a five-day group trip to places like Bermuda and Acapulco.

———

Paychex payroll services company in Rochester, NY, awards gold rings to sales reps when they've signed a career total of 300 new clients. The reps receive a diamond for the ring at 500 clients and win additional diamonds after 1,000 and 2,000 clients. Gene Polisseni, vice president for marketing, says the program rewards those who may not win annual sales contests but who consistently perform well.

———

The nine salespeople at RazorSoft International, a developer and distributor of video games in Oklahoma City, are ranked each month from 1 to 9, based on each individual's gross profit. Number 1 receives a $500 bonus (on top of commission) and the best office in the department.

———

Plant workers as well as salespeople are eligible for a bonus based on profitability and quality at Grand Rapids Spring & Wire. The size of the bonus pool is determined by profit levels and the costs of quality-assurance training time, scrap, returns and rework. The program rewards continual improvements.

———

A Victory Party is thrown for sales support staff and customer-service reps after they land a new account or meet a big deadline at Amtech, a Dallas maker of vehicle ID tags used for electronic collection at tollbooths. Chairman Michael Corboy says, "Recognition is more important than real dollars, if you pay your people well." In five years, the company has experienced growth of a surprising 8,900 percent.

———

Professional Salon Concepts, which sells hair care products and services in Joliet, IL, awards $200 gift certificates from Nordstrom's retail stores to the two sellers who "touched the biggest number of current and prospective clients" in a month. That includes the number of

> 66 Involving both customers and employees in a sales promotion makes a powerful statement about the importance of everyone in an organization. 99
>
> —BRUCE BOLGER,
> Incentive

> 66 We want all our employees world-wide to be able to win something, because we want them all to be out there actively marketing OS/2, getting excited about the product, and spreading the word about it. It would defeat the purpose to run a closed program in which there were only a few winners—it would be demotivating. We need everyone in the company to be enthusiastic about OS/2. 99
>
> —LUCY BANEY,
> Personal-Systems
> Director of
> Programming-Systems
> Market Development,
> IBM

customer classes taught, cold calls, appointments and visits.

———

IBM gets employees to help generate demand for new products by awarding medals for sales leads. Any employee who steers fifteen potential customers to an IBM dealership for a demonstration of OS/2 operating system software wins a bronze medal; additional leads earn silver and gold medals.

———

Salespeople at Octocom Systems, a maker of communications systems in Chelmsford, MA, receive a place setting of china each month for meeting their quota. Key settings (the fourth and eighth) are awarded in key sales months.

———

Chuck Piola, executive vice president of sales at NCO Financial Systems in Blue Bell, PA, tells how he started a new reward at his company for junior salespeople. "This guy was a year out of college, and one month he finally broke through—so I took him out and bought him a new suit." Piola also sometimes lends salespeople his Mercedes for a weekend so that they can see how it feels to be a top salesperson at NCO.

———

The 100 Percent Club at Minneapolis's Norwest Corporation financial services include cash, merchandise and travel prizes, but the club's recognition awards make the biggest impact on the company's more than 2,000 bankers. "Much to our surprise, the element of recognition became more important than anything else we did," says Stephen Byrnes, director of Norwest's Marketing and Product Management Division. Norwest recognizes twenty-five or so of its corporate bankers every quarter at banquets in each of the bank's ten regions. At those gatherings, corporate banking winners receive scrip worth $250 and a bronze plate decorated with the 100 Percent Club logo. They can redeem the scrip for travel and merchandise.

> 66 The best thing you can say to your workers is 'You are valuable, you are my most important asset. 99
>
> —PHYLLIS EISEN,
> Senior Policy Director,
> National Association
> of Manufacturers

Rexair in Troy, MI, offered running suits with the company logo to domestic distributors and salespeople who gave a predetermined number of in-home demonstrations of the company's cleaning system over a two-week period.

Sales employees at Citizens and Southern National Bank of South Carolina receive sales tips, "whimsical" enclosures (a football to "kick off" a program or a tape measure to "measure" achievement), as well as updates on program success.

During a recent cross-selling promotion at United Savings Bank FSB in San Francisco, customer-service and customer-relations representatives were given Hula Bucks for every

$100 in traveler's checks they cross-sold. At the end of the promotion a rally and auction was held at which they could bid on prizes, including a trip to Hawaii.

ACCO International, a Deerfield, IL, manufacturer of office products and supplies, recognizes outstanding salespeople through the President's Inner Circle, which is open to anyone who has completed one year as a commissioned salesperson in a commercial territory as a full-time direct company employee and who has reached a minimum dollar increase of 15 percent based on commissionable sales figures for the given fiscal year. The reward is a diamond-studded Inner Circle ring.

The Boise Cascade Office Products Division, headquartered in Boise, ID, annually recognizes its top thirty sales representatives with a sales executive's ring and a two-night, three-day, all-expense-paid trip to a meeting in a resort area. Recent meetings have been held in Palm Springs, San Antonio, Orlando and New Orleans.

The United Insurance Company of America's sales incentive program provides a management by objectives guide, says Richard L. Lauderdale, director of marketing sales support for the Chicago-based firm. "Every salesperson, no matter what level of performance, can select a goal to strive for within the program. The single greatest result of the program is the growth of the people who strive to achieve it."

————

Resort Condominiums International, based in Indianapolis, annually stages the RCI 500, a mock Indy 500 race in which agents compete to confirm as many time-share exchanges, sell as many subscription renewals to the company's magazine and solicit as much space reservation services business as possible. With each transaction, the representatives' paper race cars are pushed up a certain number of spaces on an oval track drawn on a bedsheet tacked on a wall. Representatives dress as race car drivers, officials or fans, and the office is decorated with streamers and checkered flags. The top producer is recognized, as are the highest-finishing Rookie of the Year, the Most Improved Driver and the three Best-Dressed Drivers.

————

Xerox Corporation, headquartered in Stamford, CT, used a sports car theme for its Fast Track sales motivation program, which also involved technical support employees and their managers. Everyone accrued points that were redeemable either for merchandise or for cash awards ranging from $10 to $10,000. Also distributed were battery-powered Ferraris and spark plugs "to spark new ideas."

————

> ❝ For some reason, there never seems to be enough recognition. After a brutal day, walk up to employees and say, 'You were great. I'm so glad about what you did today.' You'll be surprised how far a simple gesture will go. ❞
>
> —ROBERT PREZIOSI,
> President,
> Management Associates

> 66 Informal day-to-day acknowledgments mean a lot. Especially welcome are the spontaneous calls from upper management congratulating me when I exceed a sales goal. Without the personal touch, this job would just be money, and money can only motivate you so much. Recognition gives me personal pride and means something. 99
>
> —IRENE ELLIOTT,
> Account Executive,
> United Postal Savings
> Associates

Chilton Ellett, a telemarketing consultant based in Chapin, SC, suggests giving a penny for every three deals a telephone sales representative closes. The penny is then dropped into a gumball machine, and the individual is paid different amounts depending on the color of the gumball: $.25 for a white gumball, $1 for red and $10 for blue. A similar incentive used at Pacific Bell, based in San Francisco, awarded a lottery ticket for the sale of telephone features such as WATS lines, 800 numbers and call forwarding. At the end of the day the stubs were collected and the winner received a prize or cash.

———

Pentel of America in Skokie, IL, uses the Samurai Award to motivate salespeople to (1) increase sales over the previous year; (2) perform a certain amount of "end-user work," contact and sales with the final user of the company's pens; and (3) submit sales and marketing reports (SAMs) on new techniques for promoting the company's products.

Samurai winners receive a cash award, a Sales Master ring, a genuine Samurai sword and a weeklong first-class trip for two to Japan, which includes a tour of the Pentel factory as well as a ceremonial luncheon with several Japanese managers. The regional sales manager whose territory performs best in all three areas also wins a cash award, ring and trip to Japan.

———

A CASE STUDY IN SALES RECOGNITION

The FasTrack program at Morris Savings Bank, based in Morristown, NJ, rewards workers for landing new business, as well as for cross-selling to new and existing customers. Each salesperson has a quarterly quota of forty-five cross-sale points, earning a point for each additional service they sell to a customer. Tellers have a quarterly quota of fifteen referrals; when customers agree to one of their suggestions, the tellers send them over to the sales desk with a referral card. Each salesperson also gets a $2 commission for every cross-sale, and each teller receives $2 per referral. A sales coordinator tracks each person's progress on a poster in the lunchroom.

Other awards are given out at quarterly meetings. The top salesperson of the quarter and the teller with the highest number of referrals each gets $300, an extra vacation day and an engraved pewter mug. The manager of the branch with the highest deposit level gets a trophy and an engraved Cross pen, and that branch is treated to a party by the sales department.

Branch managers are eligible for bonuses as well. If 90 percent of the staff meets the quota, the managers get the same bonus as the employees. They get double that amount if all the employees attain the quota and if the branch is awarded a certain number of "mystery shopper" points from the mystery shoppers who visit each branch at least once every quarter. During those

> 66 Non-sales employees feel that the sales people are always getting the perks and they think, 'Hey, they couldn't have made all those sales without me.' 99
>
> —BOB CARLTON, Incentive Program Planner, Robert J. Young Co.

visits, salespeople are rated on five stages of selling.

In the Gold Coin Club, employees are given ten gold coins when they meet their quarterly quota; the top salesperson in each branch gets an additional five coins; five coins go to everyone in a branch where everyone meets the quota, twenty-five coins for reaching the quota in all four quarters and three coins for having a sales tip published in the newsletter. Coins are displayed on the salesperson's desk in a clear acrylic box with his or her name on it. At an awards banquet, employees use their coins to bid on prizes—including televisions and a trip to the Bahamas. The banquet features an awards ceremony modeled after the Oscars. Award categories include salesperson, teller and branch manager of the year. Winners receive SARAs (Sales and Recognition Awards), which are statuettes of "Winged Victory."

One employee who has twice been a top teller of the quarter says the program helped her. "I pay more attention to customers, and I try to offer more service, which can be more important than the product," says June Barbee, head teller at the Mendham Village branch. "And when I won the top teller award, that was really motivating."

F or meeting team goals at WFAN-FM in New York, the entire sales staff is treated to perks such as a daylong yacht cruise around Manhattan and a day in Atlantic City.

> 66 Though I'm self-motivated to a great extent, some motivation does come from outside. Recognition is great—and if the end result is a promotion, if I can further my career by being recognized as a top seller, that's great too. 99
>
> —SUSAN CHARBONEAU,
> Senior Sales
> Representative,
> United Services
> Automobile
> Association

The New York cosmetics company Elizabeth Arden implemented a sales program in which staffers who increased their sales by at least 25 percent over the same five-month period in the previous year earned a weeklong Caribbean cruise for two. Besides increasing sales, the program reduced turnover. Cynthia Bloom, resident makeup artist at Bloomingdale's in New York, says, "I've been offered jobs for more money with other companies, but I didn't take them. I'm loyal to this company— Arden's been good to me, so I'm good to them."

> **❝ Everybody works smarter when there's something in it for them. ❞**
>
> —MICHAEL LeBOEUF,
> *The Greatest Management Principles in the World*

———

At KXKT-FM, a Top 40 station in Omaha, cash, merchandise and travel are offered to sales employees. "Different people are motivated by different things, so sometimes we give them a choice," says Cathy Roach, general sales manager. "We've also done fun things, like have a wheel with cash ranging from ten dollars to one thousand dollars. For every piece of new business they brought in, they spun the wheel and won something. We've also blown up balloons containing cash and had people throw darts at them."

———

Group/Team Awards

When a team of employees achieves, the entire team needs to be recognized. If only the manager or highest performer of a group is recognized, the group is apt to lose motivation.

 **We give employees input into all of the decisions that are made so that they share in the ownership of them. That way nothing is forced on the employees because they're a part of the decision-making process. **

—DARRELL MELL,
Vice President
of Telemarketing,
Covenant House

To recognize the accomplishment of a team goal that was accomplished, Nancy Lauterbach, owner of Five Star Speakers, Trainers & Consultants in Overland Park, KS, closed down the office for a half day and took the entire staff to the movies and to a restaurant for coffee afterward. At the movie, everyone also received money for snacks. On other occasions the company offered employees a casual dress day to reward overall extra effort.

———

A manager at The Gap, Inc., headquartered in San Bruno, CA, wanted to thank everyone for working madly to meet a big deadline. She gave everyone gift certificates from a spa for a facial or a massage. "It was a much appreciated treat to help calm down and relax after a tough time," reports Carol Whittaker, another Gap manager.

———

A CASE STUDY IN GROUP MOTIVATION

When Richard Nicolosi became the head of the paper products division of Procter & Gamble, headquartered in Cincinnati, competition had taken its toll. The company's market share for disposable diapers had eroded from 75 percent to 52 percent in less than ten years. Nicolosi found a highly bureaucratic and centralized organization that was overly preoccupied with internal functional goals and projects. Almost all information about customers came through highly quantitative market research. The technical people were rewarded for cost savings; the commercial people focused on volume and share; and the two groups nearly always worked in opposition.

Nicolosi immediately began to stress the need for the division to become more creative and market-driven instead of just trying to be a low-cost producer. "I had to make it very clear," he later reported, "that the rules of the game had changed."

The new direction included much greater stress on teamwork and multiple leaders. Nicolosi pushed a strategy of using groups to manage the division and its specific products. Two months later, he and his team designated themselves the paper division's "board" and began meeting, first monthly and then weekly. The next month they established "category teams" to manage their major brand groups (diapers, tissues, towels) and started pushing

> **❝** Group incentives may be appropriate in a case where some employees are likely to try to improve their performance at the expense of other employees. Group incentives may reduce such rivalry and promote cooperation and concern for the unit's overall performance. **❞**
>
> —ROBERT D. PRITCHARD ET AL., *Personnel*

> 66 What the American worker is telling us is that the answer to increased productivity and motivation can be found inside their own companies and that meaningful rewards need to be offered to workers at every level in the organization. 99
>
> —PATRICK DELANEY,
> President,
> Society of Incentive
> Travel Executives (SITE)

responsibility down to these teams. "Shun the incremental," Nicolosi said, "and go for the leap."

A month later, Nicolosi involved himself more in certain activities. He met with the advertising agency and got to know key creative people. He asked the marketing manager of diapers to report directly to him, eliminating a layer in the hierarchy. He talked more to the people who were working on new products.

A month later, Nicolosi's board announced a new organizational structure that included not only category teams but also new-brand business teams. Within four months, the board was ready to plan an important motivational event to communicate the new paper products vision to as many people as possible. All the Cincinnati-based personnel in the paper division, as well as district management and paper plant managers—several thousand people in all—met in the local Masonic temple. Nicolosi and other board members described their vision of an organization in which "each of us is a leader." The event was videotaped, and an edited tape was sent to all sales offices and plants.

All these events helped create an entrepreneurial environment in which large numbers of people were motivated to realize the new vision. Most innovations came from people dealing with new products, but other employee initiatives were oriented more toward a functional area, and some even came from the bottom of the hierarchy. For example, a few of the division's secretaries developed a Secretaries' Network, which established subcommittees on training, on rewards and recognition and on the "secretary of the future." Echoing the sentiments of many of her peers, one paper products secretary said, "I don't see why we too can't contribute to the division's new direction."

Within four years, revenues at the paper products division were up 40 percent and profits were up 66 percent—while the company's competition continued to get tougher.

———

Northwestern Mutual Life Insurance in Milwaukee has dozens of clubs ranging from fishing and running groups to a company chorus. Retirees who continue to participate in such clubs do not have to pay dues.

———

At Ryder Systems truck rental and leasing, based in Miami, employees in quality action teams (work groups put together to come up with quality improvement suggestions) are reinforced with less tangible incentives as well as more traditional forms of appreciation. Jerry Riordan, vice president of quality, says, "We try to give them a quick response from the decision-makers, as well as quick implementation for accepted ideas. Their incentive is the pleasure of getting changes made." The company is implementing a continuous improvement process that stresses response to ideas within ten days, as well as more formal recognition and reward procedures.

———

> **❝ Our main employee incentive program has raised the average level of performance considerably. Teamwork and interdepartmental relationships have been enhanced. ❞**
>
> —DANIEL J. WILDERMUTH, Director of Marketing, Mirassou Vineyards

☞ *Send a project team on an outing (deep-sea fishing, baseball game, cruise) after completion of a project.*

MCI Communications Corporation, based in Washington, DC, had top management work together to shoot a movie. Famous scenes from movies such as *Raiders of the Lost Ark* were filmed using team members in the roles of the actors and actresses. The project served as a team-building experience. The completed movies were shown to all employees at a company meeting.

———

Small teams of food service executives received a Kodak K12 camera and a list of captions at a recent Society for Foodservice Management conference in San Francisco. After a twenty-minute lesson covering the basic points of photography, they had two hours to snap pictures to match captions such as "to boldly go" and "team spirit." Claudia O'Mahoney, executive vice president of the association, says, "The cameras made the meeting successful because they allowed people to be their most creative."

———

The most appealing motivation for team members to take on responsibility at Gencorp Automotive's new plant in Shelbyville, IN, is the autonomy granted them to determine just how they do their jobs, according to Gary J. Goberville, vice president of human resources. They have the authority to pick one of their own coworkers as their team leader. As Goberville explains, "If you want a motivated work force taking on the responsibility for good-quality products delivered on time, you have to give them the fullest authority to work out the best way to do it." Workers also determine who will be a part of their team at Worthington Industries, a steel processor and plastics manufacturer in Columbus, OH.

L ine workers assume most of the traditional personnel functions, such as hiring, training, evaluating, compensating and firing, at Johnsonville Foods in Sheboygan, WI. They also make all decisions about schedules, performance standards, assignments, budgets, quality measures and capital improvements.

Performance evaluations are made by the employees themselves. For example, three hundred wage earners fill out forms rating each other on a scale of 1 to 9 in seventeen specific areas grouped into three categories: performance, teamwork and personal development.

All final scores, with names deleted, are then passed to a profit-sharing team, which carves out five categories of performance. a small group of superior performers (about 5 percent of the total), a larger group of better-than-average workers (roughly 20 percent), an average group amounting to about 50 percent of the total work force, a below-average group of 20 percent, and a small group of poor performers who are often in some danger of losing their jobs.

The pool of profits to be shared is divided by the number of workers to find an average share, say $1,000. Members of the top group get a check for 125 percent of that amount ($1,250). Members of the next group get 110 percent ($1,100),

Tips for Building an Effective Team

✔ When hiring, look for people who work well with others. You want employees who can handle the collective process.

✔ Set a good example for your staff. For instance, leave at a reasonable hour so that they know it's OK to do the same.

✔ Encourage one-on-one discussions between staffers rather than structured meetings. Personal relationships breed trust.

✔ Hold informal retreats to foster communication and set goals.

✔ Reward collective accomplishment whenever possible, even if the reward is only juice and bagels.

PRAISE PROJECT PROGRESS

☛ *Pop in at the first meeting of a special project team and express your appreciation for their involvement.*

☛ *When a group presents an idea or suggestion, thank them for their initiative.*

☛ *Hold a lunch meeting with project teams once they have made interim findings. Express your appreciation. Encourage their continued energy. Provide the lunch.*

☛ *Send a letter to every team member at the conclusion of a project thanking them for their contribution.*

members of the large middle group get 100 percent ($1,000), and so on down to $900 and $750.

Overall satisfaction with the system is very high, partly because fellow workers invented it, administer it and constantly revise it in an effort to make it more equitable. The person currently in charge of the Johnsonville profit-sharing team is an hourly worker in the shipping department.

————

At First Chicago, the Service Products Group Performance Award is designed to develop teamwork by recognizing high-performing groups of employees each month.

The award includes a group outing—dinner, theater, a sports event—as well as a plaque for the group. All monthly winning team members attend the annual SPG Performance Banquet, at which one winner from each team is selected at random to receive a gift worth $100, and one winner receives round-trip airfare for two anywhere in the United States, plus $500.

————

At Advanced Micro Devices in Sunnyvale, CA, photos of work teams often appear in company publications.

————

At Microage Computer in Tempe, AZ, managers fine individuals who come late to company meetings and pass the money out to the people who arrive on time.

————

The aircraft engine manufacturer Pratt & Whitney, which operates primarily in Connecticut and southeastern Florida, instituted a Performance Management, Recognition and Reward (PMRR) system for organizational change. The company begins a new performance management cycle with a determination of the mission of each group or unit. Next, managers specify appropriate roles and responsibilities and set performance standards. Assessments include comments from those with whom employees have worked throughout the cycle. Criteria for leadership include the ability to empower others and recognize merit. The new PMRR process also measures each person's key job requirements and specific objectives. Pratt & Whitney has developed reward and recognition vehicles that include salary increases, verbal recognition and special cash awards. Top management was involved in implementation of the system.

☞ Create symbols of a team's work, such as T-shirts or coffee cups with a motto or logo.

☞ Ask your boss to attend a meeting with your employees during which you thank individuals and groups for their specific contributions.

☞ Cater lunches or breakfasts for high-performing groups.

Executives at JASCO Tools of Rochester, NY, made an official presentation to employees who produced the parts that won an award from Hughes Missile for quality components. The award was put on permanent display on the shop floor.

In the team program at Cal Snap & Tab in the City of Industry, CA, everyone can win, but one team wins big. "We're using a combination spoilage/attendance program," says marketing manager Richard S. Calhoun. "We put forty thousand dollars into a special fund, and every time a mistake was made, we deducted from the forty thousand dollars. We ended up giving out about seven thousand dollars." The next year the thirty-six employees were divided into four teams, with a prize kitty of $1\frac{1}{4}$ percent of shipments. One-fourth of a percent is credited to each team, and spoilage by any team member is deducted. At the end of the program, the team with the lowest spoilage also gets the leftover $\frac{1}{4}$ percent. A Chicago hospital took the same approach, creating a $100,000 cash pool that was used to satisfy billing or customer service complaints. Whatever was left in the pool at the end of the year was distributed to employees.

Team members get pins when they complete a project at the Naval Publications and Forms Center in Philadelphia. All employees also received a $500 bonus when the agency won the government's quality improvement award.

General John M. Loh, Commander of the Tactical Air Command of the U.S. Air Force, says he rewards team members who solve their problems with certificates to hang in their offices, and distributes bronze, silver and gold buttons to wear on uniforms for individual suggestions that are implemented.

William S. Ambrose, project manager and quality coordinator for the Tennessee Valley Authority, reports that the maintenance foreman at the Chickamauga Dam Reservation held a Team Appreciation Day to recognize the value of teamwork by the property maintenance crew. For lunch on that day, the foreman prepared homemade desserts.

———

Attendance and Safety Awards

Two of the most common and basic activities that companies recognize are good attendance and safety, especially in manufacturing firms. Attendance awards encourage employees to be prompt and not miss workdays. Safety awards recognize employees for following safety procedures and minimizing accidents on the job.

> 66 With so many ways to reward people, you may ask, 'How do I decide how to reward each person?' The answer is simple: Ask them. 99
>
> —MICHAEL LEBOEUF,
> *The Greatest Management Principle in the World*

General Electric, headquartered in Fairfield, CT, offers a cash bonus for every six months of perfect attendance.

The Atlantic Envelope Company in Atlanta awards employees two hours' bonus pay for every month of perfect attendance.

Copley Memorial Hospital in Aurora, IL, rewarded 128 employees with a buffet lunch, a certificate of achievement and a ceramic coffee mug inscribed with "Perfect Attendance" and the year. A special gift certificate went to the employee with the longest perfect attendance.

Pella Rolescreen Company in Pella, IA, awards a $100 savings bond to employees with one year of perfect attendance. The company, which markets windows, also arranges coffee time with top management once a year for employees with perfect attendance. It even arranged a reception with the governor of Iowa for seven employees with twenty-five years' perfect attendance.

In the Instant Win Giveaway program Todays Temporary, based in Dallas, temporary employees who have worked during the previous six months are given a card with a scratch-off panel concealing a named prize. Prizes include a diamond watch, $100 or $50 cash, calculators and six months of free long-distance telephone calls.

To recognize those who achieve perfect attendance, Merle Norman Cosmetics, based in Los Angeles, offers the following gifts:

One year: a gold engraved watch

Two years: an Atari video game, a Farberware cookware set or Oneida stainless flatware

Three years: a Toshiba personal stereo or a Panasonic portable TV

Four years: a Sunbeam or a Cuisinart food processor

Five years: a Nikon 35mm camera

> ❝ Positive reinforcement not only improves performance; it also is necessary to maintain good performance. ❞
>
> —R. W. REBER AND G. VAN GELDER, *Behavioral Insights for Supervision*

Six years: a Panasonic AM/FM stereo cassette player with two-way speakers

Seven years: an RCA 19-inch color TV

Eight years: a Panasonic microwave oven

Nine years: a specially designed ring

Ten years: a two-week, all-expense-paid trip to Hawaii for two

Fifteen years: a two-week, all-expense-paid trip to anywhere in the world for the employee and his or her spouse, relative or friend

How well do these incentives work? In a given year, more than one-tenth of all hourly employees did not have a minute of absenteeism or tardiness, and eight employees had gone ten years without missing any time from work.

———

Marion Laboratories in Kansas City, MO, gave a production worker 100 shares of stock (worth $8,000) for ten years of perfect attendance.

———

A large manufacturing firm with 7,500 hourly employees increased attendance by offering nonmonetary privileges for good attendance, combined with progressive discipline for excessive absences.

———

One company held a monthly "perfect attendance" drawing for eligible employees and awarded just $10 cash. The program resulted in a savings of more than $3,000 in sick leave, a decrease of 30.6 percent for the firm's sixty-eight employees.

———

In an effort to decrease absenteeism, New York Life Insurance Company holds a lottery for employees who have been at work every day each quarter. The first ten employees to have their names drawn earn a $200 bond; the next twenty earn a $100 bond, and seventy more receive a paid day off. A special lottery is held for employees with perfect attendance records for the entire year. Prizes are two $1,000 bonds and ten more paid days off. The company estimates that absenteeism is 21 percent lower than during the same period the previous year.

———

At Viking Freight System in Santa Clara, CA, bonuses are awarded every six months to anyone who was not absent or late more than three times and who was not involved in a preventable accident.

———

The Continental Baking Company in Schiller Park and Hodgkins, IL, recently used $50 steak gift certificates for a safety incentive campaign called Steak and Safety. Employees were rewarded for having no vehicular or personal accidents during a certain time frame. Each of twenty branches was awarded a certificate if it stayed accident-free for a given period. A lottery at each site then determined the employee who would receive the prize.

———

> **"** Well-constructed recognition settings provide the single most important opportunity to parade and reinforce the specific kinds of new behavior one hopes others will emulate. **"**
>
> —TOM PETERS,
> Author and
> Management Consultant

> 66 The recognition program, along with good training and supervision, helps keep safety on the minds of all our workers—including management and supervisors. It helps keep us focused as a team. 99
>
> —JIM RAINSBERGER, Superintendent, Pipeline Division Terminal, Quaker State

Southern New England Telephone, based in New Haven, CT, rewards employees who have driven one calendar year without a preventable accident. To be eligible, an employee must drive at least 12,000 miles annually or spend 25 percent or more of his or her work time operating or working out of a company vehicle. Employees amass certificates which are redeemed for products from one supplier.

———

Quaker State, the automobile lubricant manufacturer in Oil City, PA, has several safety recognition programs that have proved very effective. The Quarterly Group Safety Awards program involves workers as diverse as truck drivers, dispatchers, mechanics, forepersons and supervisors at the twenty Quaker State storage and distribution terminals nationwide. For each quarter without lost-time accidents, each team member earns a gift worth ten to fifteen dollars, such as a pocket knife or set of mugs, inscribed with the company logo. The program produced an increase in team camaraderie and safety awareness.

In the Safe Driving Awards program, each driver who has a twelve-month perfect safety record earns a nylon or corduroy jacket (worth about forty dollars) adorned with the Quaker State logo and a Safe Driver emblem created by an employee who won an in-house design competition. Drivers also attend a celebratory breakfast at a local restaurant and are honored in front of their peers by corporate officials. Their names are added to plaques in each terminal that commend truckers for their safe driving records. About 97 percent of participating drivers achieved safety goals in a recent year.

———

N ekoosa Paper in Port Edwards, WI, uses a committee of hourly employees who represent each department to determine the best method for recognizing safety records. Merchandise for the awards also is determined by the committee. The result is a multilevel program that rewards both long-term and short-term results. Employees receive recognition for ten or more years of accident-free service, while more frequent reinforcement of safety on the job is accomplished through monthly safety awards. Workers chosen at random are eligible for awards ranging in value from $25 to $50 for correctly answering a safety-related question.

———

A t Furst-McNess Company in Freeport, IL, which manufactures premixed animal foods, Mark S. Fryer, director of human resources, says the company gives $25 to all personnel who are assigned a company vehicle and receive no moving violations for a calendar year. If an employee goes three years without any moving violations, he or she gets an additional $100 award. Accidents with company cars have been greatly reduced.

———

Most Popular Specialty Items

✔ Wearables

✔ Writing instruments

✔ Desk and office accessories

✔ Glassware and ceramics

✔ Calendars

✔ Sporting goods

✔ Buttons, badges and ribbons

✔ Auto accessories

✔ Housewares and tools

☞ *Give an employee a day off for avoiding personal injury accidents.*

According to Dick Radell, vice president of human resources of Marcus Restaurants in Milwaukee, all the employees who work at a specific restaurant for one month without an accident are awarded a "megabuck" from the state lottery, in a program that is quite popular with employees.

———

PART III

FORMAL REWARDS

This section outlines the company-initiated formal reward programs used in many firms. Although studies show that such programs are not as motivating to individual employees as more specific, personal forms of recognition, that does not mean formal programs are not important. Such programs are useful for formally acknowledging significant accomplishments, especially as they span a long period. Formal rewards can also lend credibility to more spontaneous, informal rewards used daily by managers in an organization.

Tim Puffer, of Puffer and Associates marketing and public relations in St. Paul, describes eight general guidelines for conducting a successful rewards and recognition program: Define objectives, lead by management example, develop specific criteria, use meaningful rewards, involve employees, keep communications clear, reward teams and manage the long term.

In a recent issue of *Personnel Journal,* Philip C. Grant offered suggestions for making a rewards program work. He asserts that corporate reward systems need constant attention. The mere existence of such programs does not guarantee they will be valued or that they will have any impact on employee motivation and satisfaction. Therefore, managers must manage them. There are several ways to do so:

✔ *Tie rewards to needs.* Because each employee has different needs, reward systems must be flexible. If feasible, rewards should be adapted to each employee.

✔ *Ensure the rewards' fairness.* Every employee must understand that, in relation to the demands of the job and to what workers in similar jobs outside the company are receiving, the rewards they receive are just.

✔ *Make sure timing is proper.* It's best to schedule frequent presentations of rewards so that employees receive them shortly after the achievement being recognized.

✔ *Talk up the value of rewards.* If managers show enthusiasm for a reward at the time it's presented, they add to its perceived value.

✔ *Don't camouflage rewards.* Rewards must stand out and be highlighted; don't squeeze praise among a dozen other topics of conversation.

✔ *Present rewards in a public forum.* Rewards are not meant to be presented in the privacy of an employee's office. Schedule a special meeting for the occasion.

✔ *Don't oversell rewards.* Promote rewards, but don't oversell them. Constant talk about how great a reward is can start to make it sound ridiculous.

Multi-Level Reward Programs/ Point Systems

Most companies have one or more formal reward programs for recognizing employee performance, often integrated to address the needs of different levels and types of employees. Although such programs typically recognize only a small number of employees, for those employees the experience is significant and motivating, and the public example helps to shape the future aspirations of other employees.

"It's our business to catch employees doing something right, not wrong. The pat on the back is worth a lot more than a kick in the fanny," says Charles Nirenberg, chairman of Dairy Mart convenience stores, based in Enfield, CT. The company has incentive and recognition programs at all levels: Top executives have a stock option plan; store managers have a bonus plan, Divisional Manager of the Year and Franchisee of the Year appointees; long-term employees receive diamond-studded rings; and in-store employees who are observed going "above and beyond" win "people pleaser" buttons.

> 66 Employees will be more receptive to formal, organization-wide programs if they believe that the company really cares about them on a personal, day-to-day basis. 99
>
> —ROSALIND JEFFRIES,
> Rewards and Recognition
> Consultant

Banister Shoe in Beloit, WI, uses a combination of programs to reward and recognize employees at all levels and for various achievements. According to Claudia Cecil, director of human resources, "Different things motivate different people, so we provide a variety of forms of reward. We try to get away from the mentality that an employee should be paid more for every time he or she does something new."

Formal award programs include Manager of the Year; District Manager of the Year; the Leadership Achievement Award, also known as the "eagle ring," in which an employee first receives an onyx ring and then diamonds for it with each additional recognition; the Achievement Award, or "pyramid pen"; and the President's Club for store managers.

More informal programs include "hero meetings," which are held once a month in the central office to announce achievements; continuing encouragement to praise each other; and spontaneous standing ovations for various achievements by individuals.

CASE STUDY #1 IN FORMAL RECOGNITION PROGRAMS

Inspired by the slogan "At Ross, You're in the Company of Excellence," president Dick Gast decided that Ross Laboratories, based in Columbus, OH, needed a recognition program to enhance its tradition of superior products and services.

Inasmuch as excellence is subjective, Gast decided that an effective way to put it into more concrete terms was to allow employees to participate in the process of defining and recognizing excellence.

Gast specified that the program should be open to all 4,100 employees, from line workers to executives, and should be employee-driven. All company employees should be eligible to win and participate in selecting winners.

The program designates three levels of achievement with rising prestige and increasingly valuable awards. At each facility, the program is administered according to the number of people and their particular preferences. Any full-time Ross employee may nominate another full-time employee, whether subordinate or supervisor, for an award. Employees may even nominate themselves.

All nominations are considered by a screening committee of twelve to twenty-five workers in each area. The committee considers all nominations and selects the most deserving people to be voted on by employees in their area. Although managers can serve on the selection committee, they have no more clout than any other member in determining final selections. Service on the committee is voluntary and may not exceed two years per member.

The Award of Excellence program allows employees many chances for recognition. At the end of each quarter, the screening committee reviews all nominations submitted during that period. Nominees affirmed by the committee and verified by the personnel department as

> **66** A solid performance-improvement program pays for itself out of the profits it generates. **99**
>
> —THE MBF GROUP, INC.

employees in good standing automatically become Level I winners. Their names are announced at a general meeting, during which they receive a two-ounce silver ingot engraved with the Ross Award of Excellence logo on the front and the original Ross milk truck logo on the back. The ingot is encased in a clear plastic base and can be used as a paperweight or desk ornament. The award costs approximately $50. The number of first-time winners varies depending on the number of area workers, generally it is between ten and fifteen per quarter.

Each quarter, area employees select four Level II winners from among the Level I winners. Those four winners receive a five-ounce silver ingot with the same Level I imprints, but this time it is in the shape of an Olympic-style medal, complete with a ribbon. The award is encased in a black velvet-covered box and costs approximately $100. Level II winners also receive a letter of congratulation from the division president. At the end of the year, a recognition dinner is held at each Ross location for all Level II winners.

At the end of the fourth quarter, an election is held to select Level III winners from among the Level II winners. Level III winners get together for a three-day trip to celebrate their achievements. Activities include a visit to the company's headquarters for a reception hosted by the president, a double-decker bus tour around the city and a free afternoon, followed by a president's celebration dinner. Each Level III winner is awarded a Waterford crystal decanter with six glasses, as well as a $250 gift certificate

to be used toward his or her choice of gifts from a catalog. The estimated cost of the Level III festivities is about $20,000.

"An excellent employee is someone other employees look forward to working with because that person is pleasant, easy to get along with and does everything possible to make each working day a productive and pleasant experience for everyone," says Mike Strapp, director of marketing and financial services and Award of Excellence program chairman. "Fun is an important element in the definition of excellence.

"With any recognition program," says Strapp, "the goal is to encourage other employees to strive for the same kind of excellence as those who are recognized. Recognition from your peers is a great motivator. Recognition by one's coworkers encourages employees to aspire to personal and professional goals and thereby contribute to company goals."

"If you feel appreciated, you're going to go out of your way, too," says Marla Rossi, the company's receptionist who became one of the company's first thirty-six Level III winners. "I have always appreciated my job, but this made me feel appreciated back."

Some companies use a point system in which each worker receives 1,000 points and, subsequently, has points either added to or subtracted from his or her total. At Lavelle Aircraft Company in Philadelphia, points are subtracted from the total if the employee makes a part or

> **❝** When basic compensation is adequate, it takes something extra and something tangible to motivate people to greater performance. **❞**
>
> —*Incentive*

> **❝ When creating an incentive, managers should focus on results, not activity. ❞**
>
> —GEORGE W. WALTHER,
> President,
> Tel Excell Companies

completes an operation that causes rework, requires customer acceptance of a deviation or causes scrap. Five points are subtracted for tardiness, ten for absenteeism. For every suggestion turned in, the employee gets ten points. When a suggestion is accepted, the employee gets an additional ten points and 10 percent of the actual savings from the idea for one year. If the employee attends a training program or class, he or she can get twenty-five additional points. After four months, the employee with the most points is awarded a trip for two to one of the customers' plants, which is rewarding to employees and helps them understand the business better. The trip is for Friday through Monday.

Radisson Hotels, based in Minneapolis, have a program designed to increase employee retention and improve service. The hotels award points for being on time, providing good service to guests, improving quality in hotel operations, reaching department profit and production goals and referring new employees. The points are awarded by managers; customer service points also are tabulated from comment cards and quarterly evaluations by supervisors. Managers are rewarded for reducing turnover and costs, increasing the return rate on guest comment cards and implementing suggestions.

The highlight of the program is its prize structure. "We're offering standard merchandise prizes like TVs, toasters and golf clubs," says Sue Gordon, vice president of human resources.

But workers can also chose more practical awards such as bus passes, free child care at local day-care centers, tuition reimbursement and educational funds.

A survey of employees at Diamond Fiber Products in Thorndike, MA, indicated that 65 percent of the workers believed management did not treat them respectfully, 56 percent approached their work with pessimism and 79 percent thought they were not rewarded for a job well done.

To change these perceptions, the company developed a program called the 100 Club, which stresses attendance, punctuality and safety among the rank and file. An employee earns twenty-five points for a year of perfect attendance, twenty points for going through a year without formal disciplinary action and fifteen points for working a year without losing time to an injury. For each day or partial day of absence, the company deducts points. A worker also earns points for making a cost-saving or safety suggestion to management and for community service, such as participation in a blood drive, the United Way or Little League.

When an employee reaches 100 points, he or she gets a nylon jacket with the Diamond logo and the words "The 100 Club." The jackets mean a lot to the people who earn them. A teller at a local bank described a woman who came into the bank and modeled her baby-blue 100 Club jacket for customers and employees. She said, "My employer gave me this for doing a

> 66 Give people a chance not just to do a job but to have some impact, and they'll really respond, get on their roller skates, and race around to make sure it happens. 99
>
> —ROBERT HAUPTFUHRER, Chairman and CEO, Oryx Energy

66 Because of our incentive programs, we know that we will be here in the future and that it is because of our hard work now. 99

—CHARLES GEHL,
Coordinator,
Frank Implement Company

good job. It's the first time in the eighteen years I've been there they've recognized the things I do every day."

During those years she had earned $230,000 in wages, which had paid for cars, a home mortgage, food and other essentials, vacations and college educations. In her mind, she had provided a service for her earnings. The money wasn't recognition for her work, but the 100 Club jacket was.

In the first year of the program, the division saved $5.2 million and increased productivity 14.5 percent, and quality-related mistakes declined by 40 percent. In a new survey, 86 percent of employees reported that they thought the company and management considered them "important" or "very important"; 81 percent responded that they got "recognition by the company," and 73 percent said the company showed "concern for them as people." On average, 79 percent said their own attitude toward work quality had improved.

CASE STUDY #2 IN FORMAL RECOGNITION PROGRAMS

The MidMichigan Regional Medical Center in Midland has a number of formal recognition programs at the hospital and departmental levels, reports Marlene Perry, manager of quality management.

At the corporate level, employees, volunteers and physicians at the Medical Center can nominate another employee, volunteer or physician for an Apple Award for anything they did that went above and beyond the normal scope of their job. These nominations go to a committee to ensure that they meet established criteria. When they are approved, the nominee receives a red apple lapel pin. After an employee receives five red apples, he or she gets a silver apple; and after five silver apples, a gold apple is awarded. At the silver and gold levels there are formal presentations and gift certificates.

An employee is chosen each month as Most Valuable Person from nominations by other employees. At the end of the year, the staff is asked to vote for one of the twelve, who then becomes the Most Valuable Person of the Year. Each month the MVPs' pictures are posted at the two main entrances to the Medical Center and write-ups appear in the Medical Center newsletter and the local newspaper.

All employees are eligible for cash awards or bonuses; the difference between the two is the amount of the award. They may be given for continued outstanding performance or for a particular project.

Gift certificates can be awarded as a manager or supervisor wishes. There is no approval process. The manager or supervisor simply fills out the request and obtains the gift certificate.

At the departmental level, the Pharmacy Department has developed a Recognition Sheet that is available for anyone to complete. The Recognition Sheet has a space for an employee's name, the date, an explanation of the employee's activity or productivity and the name of the per-

> **❝ Decision-makers for the incentive programs should be very careful not to impose their own personal choices on their audience. ❞**
>
> —BRUCE TEPPER,
> Associate,
> R.W. Joselyn & Associates

son completing the sheet. The completed sheet
is routed to the manager of the department. The
Recognition Sheets are used to select an internal
Employee of the Month chosen for what he or
she did, not by the number of Recognition
Sheets that were completed. The Employee of
the Month receives a $25 gift certificate. Recog-
nition Sheets are also typed up monthly in a
summary report that is distributed at the monthly
staff meeting. At the end of the year, a contest is
held for Employee of the Year. Each of the
twelve recognized employees has his or her picture on the wall in the department, and everyone
votes. The winner receives a gift.

The Business Office keeps a Praise and
Recognition Board. Praise and Recognition
forms are available throughout the department.
Employees are encouraged to take a minute to
recognize their fellow employees for whatever
they believe warrants praise. The forms are
posted on the board if the employee chooses. All
forms go into a drawing each month; the prize is
a gift certificate. Managers have available to
them a meal ticket worth $3 that can be used for
special purposes at their discretion.

The Family Practice Center uses numerous
recognition methods. Each staff meeting starts
with recognition and thanks from the staff to
each other. When a staff person is noticed doing
something well or performing a special task, a
Family Practice Center Flower is delivered to
that person with a preprinted card from the
department. Staff lunches are also provided at
intervals as thank-yous.

The Medical Records Department has a Good

Deed Slip that employees are encouraged to fill out. Half of the slip goes to the employee, and half goes into the suggestion box. The employee with the most slips in the month becomes Employee of the Month; there is also an Employee of the Year. The majority of the positions in the Medical Records Department are now filled using an interview team. The manager and supervisors are on the team, and the remainder of the team is nominated and voted on by fellow employees. At the end of the interview process, the interview team is treated to lunch or dinner.

In the Information Resources Department, a Good News Reporter is assigned monthly. The reporter actively seeks out information about good performance by interviewing customers and peers. The reporters have been very creative and have fun with their presentations: A professional singer was brought in to sing a rap song; children were videotaped announcing the good deeds of the month in a TV news format; a *National Enquirer* format was used to spread the news; one session was modeled after the Emmys.

The Medical Center has many cross-functional and cross-departmental teams that are encouraged to celebrate their successes. Numerous departments and teams have lunches and pizza parties. After meeting for a year and a half, the Educator Resource Team had two major accomplishments. Its quarterly meeting became a surprise celebration at which each team member received a mug that said he or she was a charter member of the team. Team members also received a letter signed by the president of the

> ❝ I have one employee who won a large award and then canceled his vacation to help us out during our busy season. It does make a difference. ❞
>
> —VINCENT SCANDURM,
> Vice President,
> Sample Service Corp.

Medical Center and the chairperson for the team congratulating them on their accomplishments and teamwork. The team leaders for the subgroups also received gift certificates.

———

The Marriott Corporation, based in Washington, DC, honors fifteen to twenty people each year with its J. Willard Marriott Award of Excellence, an engraved medallion bearing Marriott's likeness and words expressing the basic values of the company: dedication, achievement, character, ideals, effort and perseverance. According to Gerald C. Baumer, vice president, employee communications and creative services, selection is based on remarks made by the nominator and the individual's length of service. Award winners represent a cross section of Marriott's work force: dishwashers, chefs, housekeepers, merchandise managers. The Marriott Award is presented at an annual awards banquet in Washington attended by honorees, spouses, nominators and top executives. "We want other employees to look up to these people," Baumer says.

Contests

One way to build anticipation and momentum in obtaining certain desired behaviors is to couch the reward in a contest of some sort. The desired behavior is typically described along with other requirements, and the rewards are made explicit. Keys to a successful employee contest include:

✔ Promoting the program and its purpose.

✔ Setting realistic, achievable and measurable goals.

✔ Limiting the contest to a short period.

✔ Keeping contest rules uncomplicated.

✔ Ensuring that prizes are desirable to employees.

✔ Linking rewards directly to performance.

✔ Giving rewards and recognition promptly.

First Security Corporation in Salt Lake City uses a quiz-show game called SuperKnow to pit teams of branch employees against each other in answering questions about the bank's products and services. The finals are televised on local TV stations, and grand prizes are awarded.

☞ *Hold a raffle for members of an outstanding work group, giving away a night on the town, a resort weekend, a home computer, etc.*

Remington Products, Inc., the personal care products maker based in Bridgeport, CT, held a company contest tied to the theme "What Makes Remington Good." Prizes included a trip to Acapulco, won by an employee who submitted a poem about the company.

Blue Cross/Blue Shield Association, headquartered in Chicago, held a contest to select employees to appear in company commercials.

Truck drivers with Viking Freight System in Santa Clara, CA, participate in truck rodeos, competing in events such as maneuvering a tractor trailer through a barrel course. Winners receive special awards such as an all-expense-paid weekend trip for two to Las Vegas or Lake Tahoe. Winners at the state finals get a free trip for two to Hawaii; national rodeo winners get either $9,000 or a new Ford car of their choice.

Hardee's Food Systems, the fast-food chain headquartered in Rocky Mount, NC, held a Competition for Excellence, in which three-person teams from each of more than 2,000 restaurants competed against other Hardee's in their districts. The teams were judged by regional managers on the three basic qualifications for fast-food employees—service, product makeup and work area cleanliness—as well as on how well they worked together.

Winning teams advanced to the regional com-

petition, and seven finalists were flown to the company's headquarters. Cash awards were given at each level, with the winners of the national competition receiving $1,500 each. All the national finalists flew in on the company jet, were whisked around the city by limousine and were generally treated like VIPs.

In a more recent competition, Bonus Bucks, employees "caught in the act of doing something right" were awarded bonus points. At the end of each quarter, each district (five to seven restaurants) held a party at which workers used their collected points to bid on items like T-shirts, televisions and VCRs.

> 66 It's not enough to tell people they should be happy to have a job here. At a time when people are asked to really stretch themselves with fewer resources, you want to reward them for that stretch. 99
>
> —BRUCE DONATUTI,
> Director of Human
> Resource Policy,
> Program Development
> and Communications,
> Citibank

For every job listing a graduate passes on to the Career Planning and Placement office at Fordham University in New York, a piece of paper bearing his or her name is entered in a lottery. A random drawing held every three months starting in October selects a winner, who is featured in the Fordham magazine. Prizes consist of season tickets to Fordham sports events, dinners at local restaurants and vacations to spots like historic Tarrytown, NY.

To promote product knowledge, Business Incentives, a Minneapolis-based performance improvement company, has foreign and domestic car salespeople call an 800 number and take a product knowledge test over the phone. During the test, a computer randomly chooses 15 to 20 questions out of a pool of about 200;

salespeople who answer 80 percent of the questions correctly win instant merchandise prizes.

———

QuizMaster, a quiz show company focused on team training based in Danbury, CT, holds contests modeled after TV game shows such as *Jeopardy; Wheel of Fortune;* and *Win, Lose, or Draw.* Contestants play in teams, usually answering questions about their company's products and operations.

———

The Domino Pizza Distribution Company, based in Ann Arbor, MI, holds an annual company-wide Olympics in which it promotes events ranging from accounting to dough making, vegetable slicing, truck loading, dough catching and tray scraping. The Olympics awards $4,000 to national champions in each of sixteen categories. The team leader who supervises the most "gold medalists" wins a free vacation.

———

The Hotel Association of New York City hosted a Hotel Olympics to recognize employees. Chefs had to prepare a Caesar salad and an appetizer of their choice; bartenders were asked to make a Manhattan and an original drink recipe; maids were timed for bed-making speed as well as tautness of the sheets; and waiters and waitresses had four minutes to carry a tray of champagne-filled glasses 800 feet, spilling as little as possible. All entrants received cash prizes,

> 66 Having an Ambassador [an employee volunteer who helps champion a reward program] gives me a set of eyes and ears at remote locations. They'll come back and tell me things like, 'You should be rewarding more employees for their efforts,' or, 'We don't want any more TVs—change the prizes.' Ambassadors are also champions of the program—they can help get people psyched up to sell more of our phone products and systems. And if one of our Ambassadors finds that motivation in his or her office is running low, he or she will tell me to hop on a plane and come out there to give them a motivational speech, a shot in the arm. 99
>
> —KEN COLLINS,
> Section Supervisor,
> Sales Promotion,
> GTE Northwest

tote bags and soft drinks. In addition, first-place winners won cameras and trips to Las Vegas and California, second-place winners received color TVs, and third-place winners got his-and-hers Bulova watches.

Cuno, a maker of water filtration and purification systems in Meriden, CT, knew wholesalers would not sell its products if they knew nothing about them. To change this, managers mailed 5,000 training guides about water quality problems with a fifty-question multiple-choice test. Wholesalers were asked to review the manual, dial a toll-free number and answer ten randomly asked questions from the list of fifty. A wholesaler who scored 80 percent or better received a customized baseball cap, a mug, a bumper sticker and a certificate naming him or her as a water filtration specialist. A total of 1,900 wholesalers enrolled, and 1,000 earned certificates.

To encourage participation, distributors who returned their enrollment cards were entered in a sweepstakes that offered eighty-two prizes, including RCA TVs and VCRs, radios and pen-and-pencil sets. The company also tracked those who did not call and encouraged them to read the manual and take the test. Once certified, wholesalers could qualify for a second-level award. Anyone who sold fifteen of the company's products in forty-five days won a nylon jacket imprinted with his or her name and the company's logo; one hundred forty jackets were distributed.

> **❝** Incentive programs can make a difference, providing visible rewards that build up confidence and knowledge. **❞**
>
> —Tom Mott,
> National Practice Leader for Sales Compensation Services,
> Hewitt Associates

Criteria for Selecting Prizes to Reward Employees

Prizes to crown an employee incentive campaign should meet most of the following criteria:

✔ Have lasting value.

✔ Reflect the effort and quality of the recipient's performance.

✔ Inspire pride of ownership.

✔ Be useful.

✔ Suit the personal taste of the recipient.

✔ Reflect the best image of the sponsor company.

Finally, the company placed fifteen "mystery" calls during the promotional period to ask distributors to name the water purification system they carried. All fifteen wholesalers answered correctly and won $100 each.

Tupperware, based in Kissimmee, FL, holds four-month "contests" and two- to three-week "challenges" throughout the year. Both reward high sales or recruiting efforts through points that can be redeemed for catalog merchandise. Meeting or exceeding sales quotas can earn dealers a week for two in Puerto Vallarta, Mexico, or a seven-day cruise.

To combat high turnover among its approximately 90,000 dealers, the company developed an incentive recruiting program. Dealers who recruit at least one new dealer in September—when turnover reaches a peak—receive a porcelain doll. Tupperware gained some 3,000 more new dealers than expected through such efforts.

Hostesses whose parties generate a minimum of $61 in party sales qualify for gifts or merchandise from the Tupperware collection. Managers who reach sales quotas or a combination of sales and dealer recruiting goals qualify for the use of a car, which can be turned in for a new model every two years, or they can choose cash.

To get them to learn the company's 1,400 types of medical tests, SmithKline Bioscience Laboratories in King of Prussia, PA, launched a product knowledge competition for its 200 salespeople. The contest had three qualifying rounds and semifinals, and then finalists from each region faced off at the company's national sales meeting. Participants received a business-card case engraved with their name and the company's logo and a gold, silver or bronze insert, depending on how well they did in each round. The seven finalists were awarded plaques, along with $150 for each gold emblem, $100 for each silver and $75 for each bronze earned on the previous tests. The overall winner received $2,000 and two runners-up received $1,000 each.

> ❝ There's nothing like a good contest to get sales cranking. ❞
>
> —TOM WEBB,
> Chief Economist,
> National Automobile
> Dealers Association

D on Lundberg, vice president and cashier of Peoples National Bank of Kewanee in Kewanee, IL, describes a contest for the marketing of new MasterCard and Visa cards in which employees receive gifts tied to the number of new accounts they open. For each of the first four accounts they open, they receive a flower; for every five additional accounts approved and opened, they win the following items in sequence: a $5 gift certificate for Dairy Queen, a waiver of card fees, a $15 gift certificate at a local restaurant, a $50 savings bond, a day off with pay, a riverboat ticket and $25 spending money.

T he E. F. Hutton Life Insurance Company, now part of Shearson Lehman Brothers, headquartered in Stamford, CT, held an offbeat sales contest called Murder in Montreux, in which marketers got monthly clues to try to determine who of eight possible suspects was guilty of a "murder." To entice marketers to play along, a special grand-prize drawing was held in Switzerland for those who solved the mystery.

————

U S Motivation, an incentives firm in Atlanta, persuaded the king and queen of Sweden to sponsor a sales contest for a group of American employees of a Swedish-owned vinyl manufacturer. During the contest, the king and queen sent the employees letters concerning royal etiquette, autographed pictures and gifts like Swedish crystal to those who were meeting their goals. At an awards dinner outside Stockholm, the king and queen presented the awards, and the ceremony was videotaped.

————

> 66 Unusual sweepstakes prizes draw an unusual degree of interest. 99
>
> —Incentive

Field Trips/ Special Events/ Travel

A significant reward in terms of cost, planning and time is a trip given to high performers in the organization. In a recent survey of American workers, 77 percent ranked a trip to a desirable destination with a spouse or guest as a positive incentive.

Travel incentive awards have a number of advantages: They are extremely desirable and promotable; they provide an exclusive venue for fostering team spirit or education; they have "bragging value" to employees; and they provide good imagery for tie-ins during the qualification period. They do, however, have disadvantages: They are too costly for many applications; travelers are out of the office during the trip; it takes extensive effort and experience to create a high-quality travel program; and typically only a few employees can win the reward.

Tina Berres Filipski, editor and director of publications for Meeting Planners International in Dallas, took her staff of eight to the Texas State Fair one Friday afternoon, paying for their admission. The field trip was not only fun, but served as a good chance to help the group get to personally know each other better.

☞ *Send the person to a health spa for a day or weekend.*

☛ *Pay all expenses for a weekend, including child care, for a deserving employee.*

☛ *Use the money that goes into the vending machines in the employee lunchroom to subsidize trips and outings.*

Jeff Alexander, a dentist in Oakland, CA, took his staff on a field trip to a shopping mall and gave each an envelope with $200 (all in ones!), stipulating that they had to buy at least five things and that any money they had left after two hours he would take back. At their next staff meeting, the employees had a show-and-tell session with their purchases.

———

Coopers & Lybrand, the consulting company, rewards its top ten professional and administrative employees with monetary awards and five-day trips to New York City.

———

Karen K. Nouchi, director of personnel and office management at the American Academy of Ophthalmology in San Fransisco, suggests offering an exceptional employee a special assignment out of the country or complimentary plane tickets for a personal trip.

———

In Tandem Computers' Outstanding Performers program (TOPS), the company (based in Cupertino, CA) awards free vacation trips to Hawaii and to such events as Mardi Gras in New Orleans and a rodeo in Calgary to about 5 percent of the employees nominated by their coworkers. Each trip is limited to fifty employees, selected to represent a cross section of the work force.

———

Mike Jay of Leadership Synergy, a medical billing company in Scottsbluff, NE, describes a sales program that strove to break past sales records for what was typically a low-selling quarter. The capstone of the program was a commitment to send the entire staff to Las Vegas for four days and three nights—all expenses paid—if certain fiscal goals were met. The goals were met and the staff had a great time, creating some company folklore and a topic of discussion for many weeks.

Digital Equipment Corporation, based in Maynard, NY, held a "Great Gatsby" event at the Empire Polo Grounds in Palm Springs for its top 4,000 sales and service performers. Arriving guests were offered champagne and treated to performances by dancing stallions and a parade of Belgian and miniature horses. Professional polo players demonstrated the rules of the sport and then competed in a private match. Drivers in period dress cruised by in a classic-car parade, followed by a dinner-dance in the rose garden.

California Leisure Consultants in Rancho Mirage offers many unique theme events. For example, Safaris Inc. re-creates Hollywood's golden age at the former home of mogul Darryl F. Zanuck. A Hollywood marquee emblazoned with the company's name greets guests; floral arrangements and candles float in the pool, and Chinese lanterns hang outside the

> ❝ If you're going to dangle something in front of them, why limit yourself to carrots? ❞
>
> —From an advertisement for Norwegian Cruise Line

☛ *For a thrilling adventure, give a skydiving package that includes a six-hour introductory course, complete with a written test and first jump. Such packages can be found all across the country at smaller airports, particularly in warmer areas such as California, Texas and southern Florida.*

poolhouse turned casino. Five hundred people can play croquet, dine, play no-stakes casino games and dance to a jazz trio at the lavish estate.

The company also arranges Indian-Western barbecues at Indian Canyon, a desert oasis with towering palms in the foothills of the Santa Rosa mountains near Palm Springs. Authentic Cahuilla Indian dancers and singers perform at the barbecue while potters, weavers and silversmiths demonstrate their crafts at an Indian marketplace where participants can shop. Stuntmen stage a gunfight, and guests—who wear cowboy hats and bandannas—two-step to a country-and-western band.

The company can arrange other events, like a "Field of Dreams" evening at Los Angeles Stadium, where retired ballplayers in vintage uniforms play ball with participants.

———

A Party To Intrigue, based in San Francisco, provides a staff of writers, producers and actors who come up with a script for a participatory murder mystery or treasure hunt. One such event was staged for a group of employees during a dinner on the Napa Valley Wine Train. The costumes, decoration of the train cars and events took participants back to the First International Wine Tasting during World War I. Another murder mystery weekend took sixty-six employees of Ford Motor Company through Chinatown, Union Square and the financial district to solve the mystery.

Mana, Allison & Associates recently closed

down Napa's Inglenook winery and staged a Renaissance Fair, barbecue and winery tours for 850 people. Mimes, jugglers and musicians entertained the group.

For a more unusual twist, Pacific Agenda took a group of several hundred people to the Hacienda Winery in Sonoma and staged an "I Love Lucy" grape-stomping competition, followed by lunch.

Brier and Dunn stages jungle theme dinners at the lions' den of the San Francisco Zoo, with lots of plants and jungle music. Brier and Dunn also arranges private yacht-club dinners, preceded by a regatta or cocktail cruise, and black-tie dinners in historic mansions; and it offers the Great American Rolling Treasure Hunt, which has teams exploring the city's neighborhoods by streetcar to discover local landmarks.

"Houseboating," according to Catherine Helshoj, director of sales for Seven Crown Resorts, based in Irvine, CA, "offers an excellent alternative to the typical resort incentive. While giving winners an opportunity to get some rest and relaxation, it also gives them a chance to see some of North America's most precious national parks."

Molson Breweries USA took 325 people from more than eighty of its distributorships across the country on a houseboat excursion. Winners attended an informal dinner with coworkers at a resort, where they were given a brief introduction to houseboat safety and handling. Then everyone headed for the houseboats, which slept

> **❝** One of the most important reasons for a company to have an incentive trip is to foster loyalty and good feeling toward the company. **❞**
>
> —JENNIFER JUERGENS,
> *Incentive*

☛ White-water rafting is popular across the country, especially in Pennsylvania, northern New York, Idaho, California, Oregon and Alaska. Give a one-day experience, a weekend camping trip, or a week-long stay at a "base camp," lodge or hotel.

☛ Sailplane or glider rides also appeal to the adventuresome, as does hot-air ballooning. These trips usually begin in the early morning and last about an hour.

from six to ten people. The next five or six days were spent meandering on a lake; optional activities, such as tours of nearby parks and group rafting, were also worked into the schedule. The last day included a Farewell Fish Fry, after which winners were shuttled back to the airport. The price for the excursion was about $300 a week per person.

Since every distributor "won" a houseboat, each decided whom to send—a salesperson and his or her family (up to six people), or a group of salespeople. Rick Clay, vice president of sales for Molson Breweries USA says, "Houseboating's a great form of relaxation because it's one of the few places where there aren't any telephones. This type of setup really allows you the opportunity to talk and listen to each other."

———

Dogsled treks across marked, groomed trails are available in different parts of the American snow belt. Lewis Elin, president of Topps Manufacturing, the maker of baseball cards in Mount Vernon, NY, has been mushing with friends, customers and suppliers for the past five years. "It gives you a totally different perspective on winter and the great outdoors," Elin reports, "while offering a really challenging experience as well."

———

For a truly unique experience—especially for car lovers—there is racing school. At Road Atlanta, a two-and-a-half-mile Grand Prix track in Braselton, GA, individuals can attend a one-

day racing school to learn handling techniques such as braking, skid padding, and heel-toe downshifting. They then spend another day racing around the track. Valvoline Oil Company organized such an incentive trip for six buyers from distributorships around the country.

———

The Travelers Corporation, the insurance company based in Hartford, CT, sends winning agents to the Masters golf tournament each year. They are flown on the company jet and wined and dined at the event. Each agent receives a bag of customized merchandise—from cookbooks to visors and suntan oil. The agents mail Masters scratch-off game cards to other key brokers, who must follow the tournament to win. Prizes range from a trip to London to imprinted visors. Richard Brown, second vice president for advertising marketing services, reports a 23 percent response rate on the card.

For nonsales employees, a putting contest is held one week before the Masters. For three days, the home office sets up a golf turf and challenges its employees to make a hole in one. Golf shirts and balls go to winners, who also are entered in a drawing for eight golf-related prizes ranging from warm-up suits to windbreakers.

———

Every dollar that marketing staffers save on airfare, hotel bills and meals while on the road earns them points toward a resort vacation for two at the Dr. Pepper/Seven-Up Companies, based in Dallas. The two people who collect the most

> **❝** If we were to put together a profile of the worker most likely to be motivated by incentive travel, it would be a twenty-four- to thirty-four-year-old nonwhite male with an income of fifteen thousand to forty thousand dollars living in the West and having a postgraduate education. **❞**
>
> —CHRISTINA LOVIO-GEORGE,
> President,
> Lovio-George, Inc.

points by year's end win the weeklong vacations. Travelers save money from their travel allotments by taking connecting rather than nonstop flights, flying on weekends, staying in more modest hotels and dining in less swanky restaurants.

————

Hewlett-Packard employees anywhere in the world may make reservations to stay, at a modest cost for a limited number of days, at any of the company's recreation areas, which include Little Basin Park in the Santa Cruz Mountains, three facilities in Colorado, one resort in the Pocono Mountains of Pennsylvania, a beach villa in Malaysia, a lake resort in Scotland and a ski-chalet complex in the German Alps.

————

Johnson Wax has nine resort facilities in different parts of the country for vacationing employees and their families, including the Lighthouse Resort in northern Wisconsin and resorts at Cape Cod and Lake Tahoe. Other companies that offer vacation spots for employees include Springs Mill, a textile manufacturer in Fort Mill, SC, and Steelcase, the office furniture maker in Grand Rapids.

————

IBM offers recreational facilities at most major company locations, including company-owned country clubs at Poughkeepsie, Sands Point and Endicott, New York, which employees can join for $5 a year.

————

Nearly 10,000 Wilmington-area employees of E. I. du Pont de Nemours belong to the company's Country Clubs, which consist of four eighteen-hole golf courses, three in Wilmington and one in nearby Newark, Delaware, as well as tennis courts and facilities for dining and social gatherings.

———

3M (Minnesota Mining and Manufacturing Company) has the Tartan Park Clubhouse, a country club in Lake Elmo, MN, exclusively for the use of 3Mers for a membership cost of $4 a year.

———

Tenneco, Inc., the pipeline operator and manufacturer of farm and construction equipment in Houston, has Tennwood, northwest of the city, which features a twenty-seven-hole golf course, a swimming pool, tennis courts, an outdoor dance floor and fishing lakes—all free to employees.

———

Individual plants at Kollmorgen Corporation, a manufacturer of electro-optical instruments, electric motors and circuit boards based in Stamford, CT, sponsor monthly outings, taking busloads of employees to Atlantic City or Great Gorge, or for daylong ocean cruises.

———

Every five years, all 1,800 employees at A-P-A Transport Corporation in North

Top Incentive Travel Destinations
(ranked in order of popularity)

———

OVERSEAS

1. France
2. Spain, England, Germany, Italy
3. Australia
4. Portugal, Monaco, Austria, Switzerland, Hong Kong
5. Ireland, Singapore, Bali, Thailand, Israel

66 Travel to exotic and/or foreign destinations is the single most sought-after prize by my sales force of 60. It gives them an escape from their normally hectic schedule and seems to make them feel that the effort they spent to get there was all worthwhile. **99**

—JOHN FRANZ,
President,
Brasseler USA Inc.

Bergen, NJ, are taken on a trip, such as an expense-paid weekend in Puerto Rico for employees and their spouses or guests.

———

All managers at Quad/Graphics, Inc., printers in Pewaukee, WI, are entitled to a free trip to New York City. The company picks up the airfare for two and provides use of the company's apartment on Fifty-seventh Street. About twenty managers a year take advantage of this opportunity.

———

Employees of Springs Mill can use company facilities (a campground, a cafeteria and a fishing pier) at Springmaid Beach in Myrtle Beach, SC, at reduced cost.

———

Steelcase, the manufacturer of office furniture, offers free camping to employees, their families and guests at Camp Swampy, a 1,700-acre recreation area sixty miles north of Grand Rapids.

———

The Carlson-Himmelman Award given by the Westin Hotels, headquartered in Seattle, is presented annually for outstanding management achievement. Recipients get a trip around the world.

———

Education/ Personal Growth/ Self-Development

Areward of additional training serves two purposes: reinforcing desired behavior and helping individuals gain skills to personally improve themselves. According to one recent survey, 87 percent of American workers believe that special training is a positive incentive and that it is deemed most meaningful by employees with postgraduate education.

Walt Disney World in Orlando, FL, offers its three-day seminar for managers to other companies. Colin Service Systems of White Plains, NY, a provider of janitorial services, is one of many companies that have sent managers to the Disney seminar as a reward.

Blanchard Training and Development of Escondido, CA, took all of its employees to the largest trade show in the training industry. Employees attended presentations, met customers and competitors and learned about the industry.

> **66** People want to learn new things, to feel they've made a contribution—that they are doing worthwhile work. Few people are motivated only by money. People want to feel that what they do makes a difference in the world. **99**
>
> —FRANCES HESSELBEIN, President, Peter F. Drucker Foundation

☛ Pay membership dues for a professional organization, such as Professional Secretaries International.

☛ Show personal interest in an employee's development and career after a special achievement, asking how you can help him or her take the next step.

☛ When an issue arises similar to one in which an employee has shown interest, involve that person in the discussion, analysis and development of recommendations.

☛ Buy the person a subscription to a magazine, journal or newsletter of his or her choice.

A CASE STUDY IN REWARDING LEARNING

At Johnsonville Foods in Sheboygan, WI, the annual across-the-board raise has been replaced with a pay-for-responsibility system. As people take on new duties—budgeting, for instance, or training—they earn additional base income. The previous system rewarded people for being present regardless of what they contributed; the new one encourages people to seek additional responsibility.

The company also uses a personal development team to help individual employees plan their career destinations and use the organization to reach their goals. Each person has an educational allowance to be used however he or she sees fit. In the beginning, some employees took cooking or sewing classes; a few took flying lessons. Over time, however, more and more of the employees have focused on job-related learning. Today more than 65 percent of all employees at Johnsonville are involved in some type of formal education.

"Helping human beings fulfill their potential is a moral responsibility, but it's also good business," CEO Ralph Stayer says. "Life is aspiration. Learning, striving people are happy people and good workers. They have initiative and imagination, and the companies they work for are rarely caught napping."

Doug Garwood, director of customer service and product management for Collins & Aikman, carpet manufacturers in Dalton, GA, reports that after eighty employees passed their GEDs (high school equivalency exams), the company hosted a graduate lunch and awarded them class rings.

Au Bon Pain, the Boston-based retail bakery, awards a $500 bonus or $1,000 scholarship toward an employee's education.

Burger King pays tuition after three months' steady work. One franchise owner paid for one course at a local college for employees who worked ten to fifteen hours per week, two courses for sixteen to twenty-five hours, and three courses for twenty-six to forty hours.

The Tacoma-based Weyerhaeuser Company, maker of disposable diapers, mounted a $100,000 Double Diaper Sweepstakes in which the company invested $25,000 in a guaranteed annuity contract in the winning child's name. Beginning at about the time of college expenses, the annuity will pay out $20,000 for five years.

Cumberland Farms, a convenience-store chain in Canton, MA, reimburses its employees for college courses.

&& Ask people what they want to do. Frequently, when a new assignment comes up, we'll give it to just the wrong person, a person who won't find it stimulating. The cure here is for management to take the time to canvass staff and match chores with interests, to the extent possible. The workplace offers so many opportunities, and when we pair them with the right people, the results are amazing. &&

—CHERYL HIGHWARDEN, Consultant, ODT Inc.

RECOGNIZE PERFORMERS WITH TRAINING

☛ Send employees to special seminars, workshops or meetings outside the company that cover topics they are interested in.

☛ Have new employees take a Dale Carnegie course that stresses attitude, people skills and customer relations.

☛ Grant all full-time employees the opportunity to attend a week-long in-house Quality College.

☛ Allow top performers to take a trip to Walt Disney World to attend Disney's People Management training program.

At Bell Labs in Murray Hill, NJ, experts on such diverse topics as bridge-building, bird navigation and whale songs speak to employees.

Northwestern Mutual Life Insurance Company in Milwaukee offers dozens of in-house training courses on subjects ranging from raising teenage children to speed-reading.

All part-time and full-time employees at Federal Express have their tuition paid.

Steelcase reimburses tuition for job-related courses.

Time Warner pays 100 percent of tuition for job-related courses and 75 percent for non-related courses at accredited institutions.

Part-time employees who have worked at least twenty hours a week for two years at the Atlanta-based restaurant chain Chick-Fil-A receive a $1,000 scholarship to the college of their choice. Four-year scholarships for $10,000 are also given. The company has awarded more than $4.5 million since the program began.

Nucor Corporation, the steel manufacturer in Charlotte, NC, offers a $1,400-a-year college scholarship to each child of an employee who has at least two years of service with the company.

———

At Odetics, Inc., the Anaheim, CA, maker of robots and spaceborne tape recorders, chairman Joel Slutzky teaches a course titled "Industry 101, or How to Start Your Own Business and Grow Gray Hair," which is open to all employees.

———

It's important to link employee incentives to the company's product. Marden Kane, a New York-based promotion firm, suggests that video camera manufacturers reward salespeople with classes on creating video productions. 3M offered hardware dealers resources in marketing, advertising and management, as did Southwestern Bell for its small business customers.

———

General Electric employees can complete a master's degree through joint programs the company has with twenty-four universities. In addition, more than 5,000 employees attend classes every year in the company's own management development school.

———

At Mary Kay Cosmetics, college tuition is reimbursed on a sliding scale: 100 percent if the employee gets an A or a B; 75 percent if he or she receives a C.

———

> **66** The message we give employees is that they're responsible for their career development, but we'll help them figure out which paths are the best for them to take. **99**
>
> —ADELLE DiGIORGIO,
> Corporate Employee
> Relations Director,
> Apple Computer, Inc.

> **66** If you believe that everyone in the organization must perform to his or her fullest potential to make the organization hum, then training—for everyone —is essential. **99**
>
> —GENERAL JOHN M. LOH,
> U.S. Air Force

> 66 Education is an essential bridge between awareness and action; it provides employees with specific tools and techniques to achieve goals. 99
>
> —From the Quality Leadership Guidelines of Baxter Healthcare Corp.

> 66 Companies that don't encourage employee education of all kinds are dumb. 99
>
> —Tom Peters, Author and Management Consultant

Polaroid, headquartered in Cambridge, MA, places an extraordinary emphasis on continuing education. It picks up 100 percent of the tuition of job-related courses taken by employees and offers more than 100 courses internally to employees.

———

Reader's Digest in Pleasantville, NY, reimburses employees 100 percent of tuition for degree or certificate programs which enhance on-the-job effectiveness, 75% for non-business related courses and programs at an accredited school, and 50% for all other educational, personal interest classes, from Weight Watchers to cooking. The company also offers wellness education seminars and exercise classes on site.

———

Every year, six to eight United States Shell Oil employees exchange positions with their counterparts in the United Kingdom through an Exchange Scientist program.

———

Pitney Bowes, based in Stamford, CT, offers courses in real estate, golf, tailoring, cake decorating, watercolor painting and photography.

———

Advancement/ Responsibility/ Visibility

A long-term reward that can be used to acknowledge the long-term efforts of an employee is a promotion or increase in responsibility. Only 22 percent of the respondents in one study believed that their organization used performance as the basis for promotion, though this practice was of high motivational importance for the respondents.

Short of a promotion, the responsibility and visibility of high achievers can easily be increased. Special assignments can be created for star performers: They can be assigned a more active role in training others, or can be sent to an advanced training class. A top performer can also serve as a liaison with home office personnel or as an adviser to other departments. If you have interdepartmental problems, concerns or projects, consider forming a task force and having your top performers represent you.

Look for every opportunity to publicize your outstanding performers to their peers. By consulting them, assigning them to special duty or giving them a prized assignment, you're saying you regard them highly. Other employees will notice and aspire to similar recognition.

If you have an in-house publication, encourage one of your top performers to write an article explaining some aspect of the business. Soon your top achievers will understand that if they excel, everyone in the company will know who they are and respect what they've done.

☛ *Give special assignments to people who have shown initiative.*

☛ *Ask an employee to help you with a project which provides a real challenge.*

☛ *Allow an employee to serve on a task force with the president of the company. In many companies, especially large ones, employees hardly ever see the president, let alone get a chance to work with him or her.*

☛ *Make responsibilities the person enjoys part of his or her job.*

☛ *Give the person more autonomy.*

☛ *Allow the person to choose his or her next work assignment.*

At Shimadza Scientific Instruments in Eldersburg, MD, outstanding performers are "promoted" to special assistant to the president for two weeks. "It's a great ego trip," reports Louis H. Ratmann, administration manager, "plus the improved understanding of the business demands is well worth it."

———

Nissan in Smyrna, TN, has a Pay for Versatility program: The more jobs a person can perform in his or her area, the more that employee gets paid. The company provides training during working hours for those interested in picking up new skills.

———

Advanta Corporation financial services in Atlanta recognizes skills (and helps develop new skills) by asking top performers to assist in training new hires and temporary employees, reports Joan Cawley, director of human resources.

———

Ladder of Success charts, mounted at cash registers, display to customers each employee's progress at Stew Leonard's dairy and food store in Norwalk, CT.

———

John Akers, former CEO of IBM, tried to find opportunities for his subordinates to present reports to higher management to get them some visibility.

———

Employees are invited to make presentations at corporate meetings at Republic Engineered Steels in Massillon, OH. Videotapes are made of the presentations, which are shown at the shareholders' meeting.

———

☛ *Let employees attend meetings in your place when you're not available.*

Stock/ Ownership

O ne of the highest forms of recognition is to treat an employee as if he or she is an owner of the company. This represents a long-term commitment to the individual, typically reserved for a select few but possibly shared with many employees. According to one recent survey of American workers, 85 percent rank stock options as a positive incentive.

The following reported exchange between Carl Buchan, founder of Lowe's Companies, the lumber and hardware supply retailer based in North Wilkesboro, NC, and a store manager on the occasion of the founder's visit to the manager's store illustrates the importance of giving employees a sense of ownership in the company.

"What is that?" said Buchan.

"It's damaged merchandise, sir."

"Look at it more closely and tell me what you see."

"Well, that's a damaged water pump, and a dented refrigerator, and windows with broken glass," replied the manager.

"That's not what I see when I look over there. What I see is money—my money—because I paid for it. And before the year is out, we're going to have a plan whereby part of that will belong to you and the other employees. Then when you look you'll see money, too, and you'll take better care of your money than you're doing now, and consequently you'll take better care of my money."

If every employee can be made to feel as if it is his or her company, pride, effort and performance will all improve as a result.

Local managers at Amoco's largest oil refinery in Texas City, TX, acknowledged they had failed to develop any sense of community among their 2,200 workers. They named Jacob Samuel coordinator of employee involvement. "I'm mainly responsible for helping workers feel they're an integral part of this business," Samuel says. "When you feel like an owner, you can't help but have more loyalty to the company."

Samuel has added a number of recognition incentives to integrate employees more closely into company—and community—life. Among them are awards for accomplishments that include improving a specific job performance, serving on a volunteer fire department, helping the underprivileged and assisting with company-sponsored events such as a marathon race, a rodeo and Little League baseball. Awards range from plaques, T-shirts and caps to TVs, watches and dinners. "They're not such big deals taken one at a time," Samuel says, "but all together they are highly motivating in helping to make our employees feel they're a real part of this plant."

At D'Agostino's supermarkets, based in New Rochelle, NY, every employee, including part-time workers and delivery staff, is eligible for the gainsharing program. The concept is simple: Stores that exceed their budgeted profit goals for the quarter share most of the excess with their employees. Gainsharing funds are allocated by department—so if the meat department pulls in 25 percent of the excess business, its employees receive proportionally more than a

> 66 Fostering empowerment and feelings of ownership results in a self-fulfilled work force that performs beyond management's expectations. 99
>
> —Finding from a survey by Quality Educational Development & Growth Dynamics

> 66 Our philosophy is to share success with the people who make it happen. It makes everybody think like an owner, which helps them build long-term relationships with customers and influences them to do things in an efficient way. 99
>
> —EMILY ERICSEN, Vice President of Human Resources, Starbucks Coffee Company

❝ Why do I work until two-thirty in the morning and then come back for a breakfast at eight o'clock almost every day? Because I own a piece of this. We've built this, and I feel a tremendous commitment to seeing it continue.❞

—A partner in Goldman Sachs

department that pulls in less. "This is an incentive to work together to improve performance and also to push each department to its potential," says Roi R. Tucker, vice president of human resources.

All employees of Tandem Computers, based in Cupertino, CA, are eligible for stock options. When stock was first publicly offered, employees were given the right to purchase 300 shares at a future date. Every year since, all employees have been given 100 share options.

At Citibank's Diners Club subsidiary, outstanding customer service can earn an employee $400 worth of stock.

At Apple Computer, based in Cupertino, CA, all employees are given the right to buy a specified number of shares of Apple stock in the future at the price the stock is selling for when the option is granted. Assembly-line workers receive options to buy 200 shares (50 a year for four years), while middle managers get options to buy from 5,000 to 20,000 shares.

Employees own a large piece of the company at Federal Express, Hallmark Cards, Linnton Plywood, Lowe's, Publix Super Markets, and Quad/Graphics.

All full-time workers who have spent at least a year at Publix Super Markets, based in Lakeland, FL, participate in an Employee Stock Ownership Plan (ESOP). Of Publix's 61,000 employees, 24,000 currently participate in the ESOP.

THE TEN LARGEST ESOPS*

Company	Business	Employees
Publix Super Markets	Supermarkets	60,000
HealthTrust	Hospital management	23,000
Avis	Rental cars	20,000
Science Applications	Research and development	11,000
EPIC Healthcare	Hospital management	10,000
Charter Medical	Hospital management	9,000
Parsons Corporation	Engineering	8,600
Weirton Steel	Steel manufacturing	8,200
Avondale Shipyards	Shipbuilding	7,500
Dan River Company	Textiles	7,000

* Employee Stock Ownership Plans (at least 20 percent majority-owned)

---

66 We believe that rewards for employees should parallel rewards that go to our shareholders. 99

—JACK L. FROST,
Senior Vice President,
Personnel,
General Mills

66 An employee of a company thinks and performs differently than someone who has ownership, or equity interest, in the company's operations. One of the reasons for Marion's continued strong performance and high productivity is that its associates participate as part-owners of the company. 99

—From the annual report of Marion Laboratories

> 66 You get a sense that you own the business. What that means is that you're going to spend a lot less time worrying about whose toes you're going to tread on and much more time worrying about how you're going to move that business forward. 99
>
> —JAMES A. MEEHAN,
> Manager,
> General Electric

Companies that participate in the profit-sharing Scanlon Plan include Dana Corporation of Toledo, OH, which manufactures and distributes components for trucks and industrial vehicles, Donnelly Mirrors in Holland, MI, and Herman Miller, furniture manufacturers in Zeeland, MI.

———

Marion Laboratories in Kansas City, MO, is one of the few companies in America that offers each employee stock options. After being with the company for one year, an employee can purchase up to 100 shares of stock at any time during the next ten years at the price it sold for on his or her first anniversary. The company's current stock-market price is prominently displayed on the receptionist's desk at all company facilities.

———

> 66 We work under a management but we are part owners. So everything doesn't come from the top down. A lot comes from the bottom up. I try to give my best. The better the company does, the more money that goes in my little kitty. 99
>
> —BILL HARRIS,
> Purchasing Agent,
> Lowe's Companies

When Carl Buchan, founder of Lowe's Companies, died his will specified that Lowe's employees, through a profit-sharing plan and trust, had the option of buying all his stock.

———

Employee/ Company Anniversaries

C elebrating anniversaries is an important way to acknowledge a long relationship between a company and an individual. Although such rewards recognize tenure rather than specific behavior or accomplishments, having long-term employees is important to most companies.

A t the Leo Burnett Company, an advertising agency headquartered in Chicago, every employee receives a gift on Anniversary Day. Gifts have included jams and jellies, a model train, statues and customized bottles of wine. In addition, every employee receives one dollar for every year of the agency's life.

———

A t Nissan, based in Smyrna, TN, any employee with twelve months of service qualifies to lease a Nissan car for $160 a month, which includes maintenance, tax, license and insurance.

———

☞ *Give all employees one rose for each year of employment on the anniversary of their hiring.*

Blanchard Training and Development in Escondido, CA, gives a company logo pin for two years with the company and a choice of engraved items, including a gold paperweight shaped like a heart. One manager buys men ties and women scarves as anniversary gifts.

———

Every Westin Hotel holds an annual banquet honoring employees with more than five years' service.

———

On their fifth anniversary with Mary Kay Cosmetics, employees receive 20 shares of stock; on their tenth, 80 shares; on their fifteenth, 120 shares.

———

NYNEX Corporation, based in New York, contracted with Tiffany & Company to develop a line of gifts for employees with five years and subsequent five-year multiples of service. While the rewards themselves foster dedication to the company, the structure of giving gifts in a series builds loyalty in a different way. For example, a Royal Limoges coffee set with an exclusive pattern designed for the company is offered at twenty-five years, matching bowls at thirty years and a matching serving set at thirty-five years. For those who want to start their collection early, a china box with the same pattern is available to five-year employees.

———

Hunter Simpson, president of Physio-Control, which manufactures medical electronics products in Redmond, WA, has lunch with the 400 employees with more than five years of service twice a year, and dinner once a year with the employees who have been with the company longer than ten years.

> ☛ Present unexpected awards at award or appreciation dinners.

The H. B. Fuller Company, a St. Paul maker of glues, adhesives and sealants, extends a special bonus vacation every five years starting on an employee's tenth anniversary. That is, at the tenth, fifteenth and twentieth year and every fifth year thereafter, a person gets an extra two weeks off with pay as well as $800 to spend on a vacation.

Employees who reach their tenth anniversary with Linclay Corporation, a real estate management and development company in St. Louis, are rewarded with memorable tributes created especially for them. "We got to a point at which we had a handful of employees who had been with the company ten years, and we wanted to do something beyond the standard plaque or wall mounting," says Mike Lee, director of human resources. "We wanted to do something personal that would acknowledge the individual contribution that each employee had made."

The gifts are determined by special committees made up of employees who know the recipients best. "Some people are easier to plan for than others," says Lee, "but usually we put together the committees two or three months

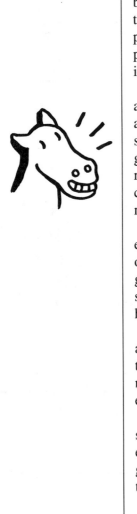

before the anniversary. The employees sometimes have an idea already, but they also get to play detective. They often interview spouses, parents, children and even neighbors to get an idea of what the employee would appreciate."

The committee, which has a budget of approximately $2,000, then decides on a gift and arranges it. Committee members take their jobs seriously. A racing enthusiast, for example, was given a portion of a limited partnership in a racehorse. A longtime bridge player got the chance to play in a major tournament as the partner of a world champion.

"Most of the gifts have been things the employees would never have spent the money on for themselves," Lee says. "For example, we gave a hunter a custom-made double-barrel shotgun. It was a luxury he couldn't justify for himself, and that made it perfect for us to do."

The gifts are presented with fanfare at cake-and-ice-cream parties attended by workers from the same facility. The parties also include the reading of a parchment proclamation, which the employee can frame and hang in his or her office.

Employees have managed to keep the gifts a secret. Lee says, "Watching the looks on employees' faces as they see what they've been given is almost as much fun for us as receiving the gifts is for them."

Whatever the individual gift, Lee says the program provides a boost for the company. "Traditional recognition programs motivate the recipients," he says, "but this program, because other employees are involved, motivates everyone."

The Walt Disney Company plans service recognition awards, peer recognition programs, attendance awards and milestone banquets for ten, fifteen and twenty years of service.

———

Mel Powell, manager of the training department for the Kellogg Company in Battle Creek, MI, converted a conference room into an office for one of his senior trainers to recognize the trainer's twenty-fifth anniversary with the company.

———

At Hallmark Cards in Kansas City, MO, employees can invite any and all of their friends throughout the company to share their twenty-fifth anniversary cake. Typically 200 to 1,000 people show up for each celebration.

———

Pitney Bowes, headquartered in Stamford, CT, has an anniversary vacation policy that gives an employee with twenty-five years of service an extra month's vacation. The same benefit is then offered to the employee every fifth year.

———

When Raychem Corporation, based in Menlo Park, CA, was twenty-five years old, it held a gigantic community party to which it invited all its employees and their families, as well as special guests. The maker of high-tech industrial products held a daylong celebration at its 140-acre plant site. Everyone was served a

> **❝ A corporate award is like getting a medal. It is the honor of recognition for outstanding achievement. ❞**
>
> —From an advertisement by Longines-Wittnauer Watch Company

☞ Engrave on a plaque the names of employees who have reached ten, fifteen, twenty or more years of service. Acknowledge individual achievements during a company meeting each quarter.

steak dinner. There was continuous entertainment for seven hours, featuring headline acts and fifteen carnival rides, including a Ferris wheel and a merry-go-round.

———

The J. C. Penney store in Laurel, MT, had a twenty-fifth-anniversary sale to honor Pat Mullaney, who had managed the store for twenty-five years.

———

When Baxter Healthcare Corporation had its fiftieth birthday, fifty rank-and-file employee ambassadors from fifty facilities in eighteen counties traveled to the Deerfield, IL, headquarters to mark the occasion.

———

For Ryder Systems' fiftieth-anniversary celebration, employees shared a cake that was shaped like a truck and covered with yellow icing.

———

To mark the seventieth anniversary of a British subsidiary, Johnson Wax closed its Racine, WI, plant for a week, chartered a Boeing 747 jet, and flew the entire British work force—480 people—to the United States, where they were put up in hotels, toured the company's facilities, shopped and enjoyed a banquet. One night employees in Racine picked up the British guests and brought them to their homes for dinner. The visitors also spent two days sight-

seeing in New York City and had dinner at the
World Trade Center.

———

When Beneficial Management Corporation
of America, based in Peapack, NJ, celebrated its seventy-fifth anniversary, the company
wanted to produce a sizable increase in sales. To
gain an extra edge, management decided to
stimulate three levels of employees—branch
associates, branch managers and district/regional
supervisors—with a merchandise incentive.
Employees who achieved their goals won their
choice of top-end merchandise from an attrac-
tive catalog. The company also promised to
enter all participants in a drawing for prizes. A
full 98 percent of the target audience signed up
for the "Celebration Continues" campaign, and
the insurance company's sales jumped 31 percent over a twelve-month period.

———

Benefits/ Health/Fitness

I f you give the same awards or privileges to all employees, such recognition may not be considered a motivator, in that it is not individually oriented to specific achievements or performance. In fact, a gift made to everyone may serve to de-motivate high performers in your organization, who see others getting the same reward. Still, certain benefits, or the overall benefits package, can be an important part of what attracts performers to your company. All employees need benefits such as medical coverage, and the combination of benefits is often a significant factor in their initial selection of the organization.

The Leo Burnett Company, the largest ad agency in Chicago, keeps a bowl of red apples in the reception rooms on every one of the eleven floors the company occupies. Burnett gives away 1,000 apples daily.

Hewlett-Packard, headquartered in Palo Alto, CA, offers free refreshments, as does Hallmark Cards, Inc., in Kansas City, MO.

All 6,000 employees at the main branch of J. P. Morgan & Co. in New York get a free lunch every day. The perk costs the financial services holding company $8 million a year. Employees of Northwestern Mutual Life Insurance, based in Milwaukee, also get lunch, which costs that company about $3 million a year.

———

A chef prepares a seven-course lunch daily for employees of Merle Norman Cosmetics, based in Los Angeles, at a cost to the employee of 25 cents. There is no charge for snacks and beverages, which are spread out in the company dining room during morning and afternoon breaks. In the morning, employees can choose among muffins, pastries and croissants, and in the afternoon they can pick from an assortment of pies or cakes, doughnuts, cookies and ice cream.

———

E mployees of Saga Corporation food service in Menlo Park, CA, receive free lunches. Lunches are subsidized at Mary Kay Cosmetics, where a hot meal costs less than $3. Each table has a white cloth and a vase of flowers. Employees may choose from a variety of cold and hot lunches, including a complete "Lite Line" selection menu for as little as $2.20 at Reader's Digest. The company also offers the convenience of a daily "take-out" dinner. Springs Industries, Inc., based in Fort Mill, SC, offers low-cost hot meals at most of its plants for all three shifts.

———

Q uill Corporation office supplies and equipment in Lincolnshire, IL, tries to lower health care costs by rewarding employees. The company estimates its health care costs for six months and places the money in a pool. If funds

> 66 ROLM recognizes that people are the greatest asset. There is no 'us' and 'them' attitude here; everyone is important. Upper management is visible and accessible. There is always time to talk, to find solutions and to implement changes. 99
>
> —ANDREA NIEMAN,
> Administrative Assistant,
> ROLM Corporation

remain in the pool at the end of the six months, they are divided equally among participating employees. Health care costs for the company have declined approximately 35 percent in each of the first two years of the program.

———

Everyone who works for Anheuser-Busch Companies, based in St. Louis, is entitled to two free cases of beer a month.

———

At Apple Computer, based in Cupertino, CA, all employees—from assembly-line workers to vice presidents—are loaned a computer just two months after joining the company in a program called Loan to Own. Ten months later the computer is theirs, no strings attached. One Christmas all employees received a solar-powered calculator; the next year they received an AM/FM radio with headphones.

———

Many firms reward employees with the use of the company's own products:

General Cinema: $1 movie passes for employees and their guests

Mirage Resort: free tickets to Las Vegas shows; free lunch at the hotel's dining room once a month

Southwest Airlines: free standby air travel for employees and their families

Ben & Jerry's: three pints of ice cream for every worker

———

At Exxon, employees get a 10 percent reduction in the price of Exxon gas and 15 percent off the price of TBA (tires, batteries and accessories) from Exxon service stations. Gas is also sold at cost at Federal Express, Liebert Corporation, Linnton Plywood and Merle Norman Cosmetics, which also sells its employees the cosmetics it manufacturers at cost.

———

At Delta Airlines, employees and their spouses receive annual passes good for unlimited travel anywhere on the Delta system, and reduced rates on other airlines after ten years of service.

———

Employees at Federal Express can fly free on the company's planes and at reduced rates on other airlines.

———

At Rainer Bancorporation in Seattle, employees get two free personal checking accounts, free checks, money orders and cashier's checks without service charges, traveler's checks with no commission, Visa accounts at reduced rates, bank and government securities available for purchase at a reduced fee, discounts on loans, and reduced rates for trust department services.

———

Random House offers all employees ten free books a year and the right to buy any other Random House book at a 50 percent discount.

———

> **❝** We want people who enjoy what they're doing and for whom work is an extension of themselves. **❞**
>
> —EMILY ERICSEN,
> Vice President
> of Human Resources,
> Starbucks Coffee Company

> 66 Workers have always known how to work smarter, and when management isn't watching, they do. They then use the time to create a halfway pleasant social experience— discussing last Sunday's football game or Betsy's wedding shower or just working at an easier pace. If companies want people to give that up, they're going to have to offer something valuable in trade— something that meets basic human needs for social interaction and financial well-being. 99
>
> —JOHN ZALUSKY, Economist, AFL-CIO

At Nissan, office and factory employees are each provided with three changes of work clothes at no expense. Wearing the work clothes is strictly voluntary.

In its Dallas plant, Mary Kay Cosmetics provides each production-line worker with three sets of work clothes a year. Women get a bright red jumpsuit as well as reddish outfits with printed blouses and slacks. Men wear blue trousers and shirts and matching baseball caps.

Retired employees of H. B. Fuller Company, a maker of glues, adhesives and sealants based in St. Paul, have the first shot at part-time openings and special projects.

Leo Burnett provides up to $3,000 in adoption assistance; H. B. Fuller, Herman Miller and Physio-Control provide $1,500; IBM and Procter & Gamble provide $1,000. Security Pacific Corportation, based in Los Angeles, offers adoption aid equal to maternity support.

Close to a thousand firms in the New York metropolitan area pass out TransitCheks to their employees to be used for buses, subways, ferries and commuter railroads. Champion International Corporation in Stamford, CT, offers $15 a month to van-poolers and also buys TransitCheks. Vice president of corporate facilities

Terry Wurtzbacher says about 20 percent of employees who drove to work alone now use car pools, van-pools or mass transit. Interstate Electronics in Anaheim, CA, gives $20 a month to each person in a car pool and the same amount to employees who take the train from San Diego. Xerox Corporation in Stamford, CT, also gives workers discounts off monthly bus or train passes, subsidizes van-pools and provides preferential parking for car pools and van-pools.

P hysio-Control Corporation subsidizes a bus service during off hours on Fridays and weekends for employees who are working odd shifts.

R eader's Digest subsidizes employee van-pools. Employees also can identify potential car or van-pools in their areas through a computer access program which matches employee's transportation needs.

B axter Healthcare Corporation, which sells health care products, systems and services, picks up one-third of the day-care costs for its employees at two day-care centers near its Deerfield, IL, headquarters.

S ecurity Pacific employs two social workers to answer a toll-free number and talk with employees who are having personal problems.

A Sampling of Benefits Offered by Time Inc.

✔ If employees work past 8 P.M. in New York, they not only get $10 toward dinner, but also the right to take a cab all the way home—even to New Jersey.

✔ Employees get free copies of all Time Inc. magazines.

✔ Fathers or mothers get parental leave up to one year.

✔ Employees get free admission to the major museums in New York City.

✔ After five years of service, employees get free physical exams.

The company will pay for up to a year's worth of counseling for employees.

———

Odetics, a maker of robots and spaceborne tape recorders, rents the South Coast Repertory Theater—the largest performance space in Orange County, CA—each year for employee productions.

———

Tenneco, Inc., the Houston-based pipeline operator and manufacturer of farm and construction equipment, has a large fleet of vans to pick up employees, covers most of the cost for monthly bus passes and subsidizes parking expenses for car pools. The Tenneco health and fitness facility provides all the clothing employees need for a workout, including socks and athletic supporters.

———

IBM provides health classes and physical examinations.

———

Employees at Johnson & Johnson have access to a large fitness center that includes a comprehensive program in which enrollees undergo a physical examination and then have professionals guide them in a physical fitness regimen. Other companies known for their fitness centers include ROLM in Santa Clara, CA, Springs Industries, Inc., and Tenneco, Inc.

———

As an incentive for staying healthy, Johnson Wax deposits $300 in every employee's flexible health plan at the beginning of each year to be used to pay for health care charges not covered by the company's health plan. Unused money in the account at the end of the year is paid to the employee in cash.

"It is not the dollar cost of the award, but sometimes the novelty of it," says Terry L. Curry, manager of human resources for Muscatine Power and Water in Muscatine, IA. Employees there take part in two rounds of "wellness" team events during the summer. First-round participants receive T-shirts. If employees participate in both rounds they also receive shoelaces. The company has also given away stadium cushions for participation in late-summer or early-fall wellness events.

Mesa, the Dallas oil company, gives workers up to $700 a year in bonuses if they exercise three times a week, don't smoke, don't take sick days and don't submit major medical claims. Since the program started, the company has cut health care costs to 25 percent below the industry average.

Westinghouse in Pittsburgh gives $200 annual bonuses to workers who do ten minutes of aerobic exercise three times a week

> **66** An employee with a good family life is healthier and more productive. **99**
>
> —SYLVIA SEPIELLI, Incentive Program Designer, Hyatt Hotels

Most Unusual Benefits

✔ Free taxi ride home—Time Inc.

✔ Free Saturday night movies— Merle Norman Cosmetics

✔ First-class air travel—Leo Burnett

✔ Free airline passes—Delta

✔ Fridays off in May —Reader's Digest

✔ Paid week off at Christmas— Northrop

✔ Free home computer—Apple Computer

✔ Free Lunch— Hewitt Associates, J.P. Morgan

✔ Leased automobile —Nissan

—ROBERT LEVERING, MILTON MOSKOWITZ and MICHAEL KATZ, *The 100 Best Companies to Work for in America*

for at least nine months a year. The company estimates it saves $1,715 annually on every fit versus unfit employee.

———

Gail Sneed, resource coordinator for the City of Dallas, suggests offering a Free Month of Wellness for employees who otherwise must pay to use fitness equipment and take classes.

———

Reader's Digest reimburses up to 50% (up to $250/year) of the cost of health club memberships for its employees. Employees who choose to take sports instructions or participate in a sport can also be reimbursed for part of these fees. Time Inc. does the same if the club has a cardiovascular fitness program.

———

Steelcase, Inc., based in Grand Rapids, has a minihospital staffed by nineteen nurses and two physicians. The company also employs a psychologist and two social workers to counsel people on their personal problems, for free, on company time or after hours.

———

REI (Recreational Equipment, Inc.), based in Seattle, allows employees to use rental equipment, if available, for free.

———

Viking Freight System, based in Santa Clara, CA, equips its trucks with AM/FM radios

and cassette decks. Viking also provides off-duty rooms for drivers, with pool tables, video games and color TVs with VCRs.

———

Most employees of Westin Hotels receive free meals while at work. Free rooms are also available to employees after one year's service. A ten-year employee and his immediate family can stay for fifteen nights at a Westin Hotel, with 20 percent off the cost of meals. Other employees get 50 percent off any hotel room rate.

———

Production workers at Worthington Industries, the steel processor and plastic products manufacturer in Columbus, OH, can get $2 haircuts on company time at barbershops in the plants. Employees can also fish for bass and bluegill during their off-hours at a stocked pond near the corporate headquarters.

———

Southern California Edison has twelve staff physicians and part-time specialists to take care of its employees. The company also gives employees 25 percent off their electric bill.

———

Employees are offered selections from a gift catalog in lieu of a year-end bonus on alternate years at Hatfield Quality Meats in Hatfield,

> 66 It's not the gift itself but the idea behind it. It's nice to walk around the house and see an item and think, 'Oh, yeah, that's from 1984; I remember what I did for that one.' The memory the item gives you is so much better than money. Cash is here today, then it's gone. 99
>
> —BARION MILLS, JR.,
> Agency Manager,
> State Farm Insurance

PA. Every employee receives the same gift amount and can select an expensive item or several less expensive ones.

————

The Southern Baptist Foreign Mission Board in Richmond, VA, gives all employees a card with candy at Thanksgiving. The gifts are delivered by managers carrying baskets. "People get so much at Christmastime," says Charlene Eshleman, staff development manager, "that this gift is more special."

————

Each Christmas Remington Products gives out a turkey, and each year another item is added—cranberry sauce, stuffing mix, a coupon for a bottle of wine—all bagged by Remington executives.

————

Charity/Social Responsibility

Employees appreciate companies that value their efforts in supporting charities and local government. Such behavior reflects positively both on the individual and on the organization.

The Levi Strauss Foundation makes a donation of $500 to community organizations in which an employee actively participates for a year. If an employee serves on the board of a nonprofit organization, the company will give that organization a grant of $500 if the organization has a budget of up to $100,000, $1,000 for a budget between $100,000 and $1 million, $1,500 for budgets more than $1 million.

At Atlantic Richfield Company (ARCO), headquartered in Los Angeles, annual community service awards go to employees who have made outstanding contributions in the community; the company matches two for one any employee's or retiree's donation to a social service organization or college.

> **❝** [When company executives get involved in charity work] it sends the message that the leaders are invested in their community, that there's more to life than making a profit and that they care about their employees having balanced lives. **❞**
>
> —Dr. Ann McGee-Cooper, Consultant

☛ Give a department
a day off to work in a
homeless shelter or help
clean up a local park.

☛ Give employees time
off to give blood.

☛ Match donations to
an employee's college of
choice.

☛ Make a donation in
the name of an employ-
ee to the charity of his
or her choice.

At D.D.B. Needham Worldwide, a New York-based advertising agency, employees are given time off to work in community service or on political campaigns.

———

At McCormick & Company, Inc., a manufacturer of seasonings, spices and frozen foods based in Baltimore, employees are encouraged to work one Saturday each year, designated Charity Day. Employees donate their pay for the day at time and a half to a charity, and the company matches their earnings dollar for dollar. More than 90 percent of employees participate.

———

The Thurston-Dupar Inspirational Award is given by each Westin Hotel to employees who have not only excelled in their jobs but also made important contributions in community service. A company-wide winner is then selected to receive a two-week, expense-paid vacation for two at a Westin Hotel, $1,000 in cash, as well as airfare and expenses to attend the announcement ceremonies at the annual management conference.

———

State Farm Insurance Company donated money to the Special Olympics based on agents' producing certain sales levels in one incentive program, and donated money to the Statue of Liberty restoration in another.

———

Saskatchewan Telecommunications raffles off merchandise prizes to employees and others and places the proceeds in a Help Our Own People fund for employees who need special medical attention. So far ten employees have made use of the fund, which raised as much as $23,000 in its first year.

———

Reader's Digest sets aside space for employees' gardens and plows and fertilizes the land for a nominal cost. Control Data Corporation in Minneapolis also has plots where employees can grow their own vegetables.

———

Cato Johnson, a promotion agency in Lombard, IL, offers an Adopt-A-Tree America kit which contains everything needed to plant a tree in one's backyard: a fertilizing peat pellet, a packet of seeds, gravel and instructions. The species of tree is selected according to geographic region.

———

Appendix I

Where to Get Specialty Reward Items

Action Images
1892 First St., Ste. 101, Highland, IL 60035. Published a color poster depicting statistics and program-cover art from every Major League Baseball All-Star Game going back to its inception in 1933

American Express
Corporate Sales, 4315 South 2700 W., Rm. 3520, Salt Lake City, UT 84184, (800) 666-7317. The American Express Gift Cheque is an impressive award that offers the flexibility of cash

American Tool Companies Inc.
John Robert or Deb Schwan, 108 S. Pear St., DeWitt, NE 68341, (402) 683-2315 or (800) 838-7845. Sells tools and tool sets that can be custom imprinted, including Vise-Grip locking hand tools

Bennett Brothers, Inc.
30 East Adams Street, Chicago, IL 60603, (312) 263-4800, Web site www.bennettbros.com Offers an annual catalogue, Choose-Your-Gift and Prize Book with 50+ gifts that can be customized in each of 13 price levels from $16 to $1,000

Bill Sims Company
102 Lake Vista Drive, Chapin, SC 29036, (800) 690-1860. E-mail bill2billsimms.com; Web site www.safetyonline.net/ billsims Offers tax-free scratch-off Star Bucks. Award your performers with Star Bucks that can be redeemed for 1,000's of gifts. Also offers custom support posters, newsletters and promotional logo'd gifts

Brielle Galleries
Sharon Miller, 707 Union Avenue, P.O. Box 475-V, Brielle, NJ 08730-0475, (800) 631-2156 or (908) 528-8400. Twelve long-stemmed chocolate roses with silk leaves, packaged in a gold florist's box with red bow

Bulova Corporation
National Sales Manager, Special Markets Division, One Bulova Avenue, Woodside, NY 11377-7874, (718) 204-4600 or (800) 423-3553. Offers solid brass miniature replicas of world-famous clocks and customized watches that you can

add diamonds to as an award—one diamond at a time—by sending it back to Bulova

California Awards and Designs, Inc.
925 Wilshire Blvd., Suite A, Santa Monica, CA 90401, (310) 656-0779, (310) 656-0798, FAX (310) 656-0798, Web site http://www.ca-designs-awards.com Quality crystal awards: engraved, laminated and cast plaques; trophies, medallions and unique gifts supplied with excellent service. Manufacturers of the engraved business card paperweight. Custom orders welcomed

Creative Cakery
636 Redondo Ave., Long Beach, CA 90814, (310) 438-2301, (800) 482-5994, ext. 8079. Customizes baked goods—bundt cakes decorated with ribbons, bows, balloons, flowers. Ship nationwide

Dartnell Corporation
4660 N. Ravenwood Ave. Chicago, IL 60640, (800) 621-5463, FAX (800) 327-8635, Web site www.

dartnellcorp.com Sells the spiral-bound Dartnell Desk Planner which can be custom imprinted in 24-karat gold

Eastman Kodak
343 State Street, Rochester, NY 14650-0519, (716) 724-4000. Presents its newest Fun Saver disposable camera, the Telefoto 35, which has a telephoto lens and high-speed film. Offers the basic Fun Saver 35, an upgraded version with flash, the water-resistant Fun Saver, and a panoramic model that produces wide-angle pictures

Entertainment Research Group
497 Walnut St., Napa, CA 94559, (707) 253-1592. Offers six-foot-tall inflatable costume characters for meetings, conventions and trade shows

Express Visa Service
2150 Wisconsin Ave., Ste. 20, Washington, DC 20007, (202) 337-2442, FAX (202) 337-3019. Visa and passport services;

provides legalization services

Fighter Pilots USA
P.O. Box 3488, Barrington, IL 60011, (800) 56-TOP-GUN. E-mail fpusa@concentric.net; Web site http://wwwtravelassist.com/tcd/fighter Customers actually fly fighter jets and engage in aerial combat maneuvers. Mission includes one hour of ground school, one hour of combat flying and a one-hour debriefing that includes photos and videos of the flight

Fortune Cookie Division
Wonton Food Inc., 220-222 Moore Street, Brooklyn, NY 11206, (718) 628-6868, Web site wontonfoods.com Offers fortune cookies with personalized messages in several flavors

Fotoshow Inc.
1767 Irving Ave., So., Minneapolis, MN 55403, (612) 377-4531. Call or write for a photo organizer, featuring eight see-through

compartments that can house a total of 400 prints. The unit, set in a black plastic base, can also store baseball cards, recipe cards or other documents

Franklin Electronic Publishers

I Franklin Plaza, Burlington, NJ 08016, (609) 386-2500, Web site www.franklin.com New Big League Baseball Electronic Encyclopedia contains more than one million statistics on the sport. Also sells Crosswords, an electronic crossword-puzzle aid

Frazier & Hoyt Incentives

Frazier & Hoyt Incentive Group, 1801 Hollis St., Ste. 1010, Halifax, NS, Canada B3J3N4, (902) 421-1113, FAX (902) 425-3756, Web site www.frazierhoyt. com
Insurance company

Gingess Formalwear

180 N. LaSalle St., Chicago, IL 60601, (312) 236-2333, FAX (312) 580-7170. Tuxedo and formal wear rental and service

G. Neil Companies

720 International Parkway, P.O. Box 450939, Sunrise, FL 33345-0930, (954) 846-8899, Web site www.gneil.com/rh/ Personalized certificates, plaques, frames and presentation folders

Fontazzi

P.O. Box 18612, Irvine, CA 92623, (800) 428-0522. Will custom imprint gourmet popcorn tins and gift baskets

Haas-Jordan Company

1447 Summit Street, P.O. Box 1596, Toledo, OH 43603, (800) 536-0283 or (419) 243-2189. Sells a personal beach umbrella imprinted with your company logo

Harry and David

Business Division, Medford, OR 97501, (800) 248-5567, Web site harryanddavid.com Offers rewards from fresh fruits and meats to savory seafood and gift baskets

Heritage Promotions, Inc.

1076 Pebble Creek Dr., Elsmere, KY 41018, (606) 342-4171. Motivational posters, t-shirts, lapel pins, bumper stickers, labels, pen-pencil sets with logo, corporate blazers

Hertz Corp.

225 Brae Blvd., Park Ridge, NJ 07656, (201) 307-2301, Web site www.hertz.com Offers Award Check Vouchers good for car rentals, starting at $25

Hillerich & Bradsby Company

Premium and Incentive Dept., P.O. Box 35700, Louisville, KY 40232, (502) 585-5226 or (800) 282-2287, Web site www.slugger.com Offers sporting equipment that can be custom printed with your company name, logo, individual's name or promotional message, including baseball bats, baseball gloves and golf clubs

Hinda Incentives

2440 West 34th St., Chicago, IL 60608, (773) 890-5900, FAX

(773) 890-4606, Web site www.hinda.com A full-service incentive company with in-house program administrators, creative and marketing professionals and merchandise recommendation and sourcing

Historic Newspaper Archives
Dept. P, 1582 Hart St., Rahway, NJ 07065, (800) 221-3221, Web site historicnewspaper. com Original U.S. newspapers dating back to 1880. Encased in personalized gold-embossed binder with certificate of authenticity

HL Golf Products
777 Marlborough Dr., Detroit, MI 48215, (800) 999-5448. Features the HL Shoebag with a separate compartment for each golf shoe and shoebrush, shoehorn, socks, powder and other accessories

Houghton Mifflin Company
222 Berkeley, Boston, MA 02116, (617) 351-5000, Web site www.hmco.com Offers books that can be customized with a personal message, company logo or custom title

Irwin Productions
Cheryl Irwin, 6211 Yarrow Dr., Ste. B, Carlsbad, CA 92009, (619) 931-1103. Offers an Escapade show of singers and dancers who interact with the audience. The theme can be tailored to any corporate event

JCPenney
Incentive Sales, 9701 W. Higgins Rd., Ste. 400, Rosemont, IL 60018, (800) 832-4438, Web site jcpenneyincentives.com Gift certificates good at all retail stores and through all catalogs

Jet Lag Watch Company
1193 Walnut St., Ste. 8, Newton Highlands, MA 02161, (617) 630-0024. Offers a watch that lets the user adapt naturally to a new time zone by running more slowly or more quickly during a flight

John's Inc.
800 W. Johns Rd.,
Apopka, FL 32703, (407) 886-8850. Growing gifts—live plants in pots that can be customized with your name or company logo. Minimum order of 200 pieces

Kirk Stieff Company
Baltimore, MD, (410) 338-6080. Creates art and sculpture

Kmart Corporation
Sheena MacDonald, Gift Certificate Administration, 3100 W. Big Beaver Rd., Troy, MI 48084, (800) 345-2497 or (313) 643-2560. Personalized gift certificates in any denomination between $5 and $250

Lalique Crystal
Special Markets Division, 41 Madison Avenue, New York, NY 10010, (212) 684-6338. A collection of crystal vases, perfume bottles, objects d'art and bases for award presentations that can be customized

Legal Sea Foods
33 Everett St., Boston, MA 02134, (800) 343-5804 or (617) 254-7000. Offers

lobsters, clams, steaks, other delicacies, and custom-imprinted lobster pots

Legends
11908 Ventura Blvd., Studio City, CA 91604, (800) 726-9660 or (805) 520-9660, Web site legends@aol.com Supplies fine-art sculptures in bronze, pewter, brass vermeil, and 24-karat gold vermeil

London Fog
Londontown Corporation, Londontown Boulevard, Eldersburg, MD 21784, (410) 795-5900. Rainwear, outerwear, blazers, and sweaters

Lonestar
920 S. Oyster Bay Rd., Hicksville, NY 11801, FAX (516) 939-2834. Catalogue of products including Karaoke machines, stylized telephones, answering machines and calculators that can be customized

Mc Arthur Towels
700 Moore St., P.O. Box 448, Baraboo, WI 53913, (800) 356-9168 or (608) 356-8922. Imprintable towels and robes

Marketing Innovators
9701 W. Higgins Rd., Rosemont, IL 60018, (847) 696-1111, Web site marketinginnovators.com Freedom to Choose® retail gift certificates

Media Systems, Inc.
727 Wainee St., Ste. 201, Lahaina, HI 96761, (800) 398-2271, Web site http://www. mediasys.com Photography, video and computer graphics

Multi Image Productions
8849 Complex Dr., San Diego, CA 92123, (619) 560-8383, Web site www.multiimage. com Produce custom multimedia shows

Name Event Sunglasses
32178 West Highway K, Hartland, WI 53029, (414) 369-5633. Offers 13 styles of sunglasses with your name, slogan or logo

NBA Properties
John Killen, NBA Properties Premium Department, 6454 Fifth Avenue, New York, NY 10022, (212) 826-7000, Web

site www.nba.com The first-ever NBA premium catalogue. Merchandise—from pens and key chains to apparel and sporting goods—with an NBA team name and logo

NordicTrack
104 Peavey Rd., Chaska, MN 55318, (800) 328-5888, Web site www. nordictrack.com Features the new Back & Stomach Machine—a seat that rotates to exercise back, abdominals and obliques

Omaha Steaks
Incentive Sales Department, Dept. WB2011, P.O. Box 3300, Omaha, NE 68103, (800) 228-2480, Web site http://www. omahasteaks.com Sample packages of steaks, all cuts

Oneida Silversmiths
Oneida Planning Guide, Oneida, NY 13421-2829, (315) 361-3343. A catalogue of gifts from $50-$100 that can be personalized

Orrefors Kosta Boda
Special Markets Group, 140 Bradford Drive,

Bretlin, NJ 08009, (800) 433-4167. Hand-crafted crystal awards that can be personalized

Panasonic
Premium Sales Division, 1 Panasonic Way, Secaucus, NJ 07094, (201) 392-6198. More than 400 electronic products from microwave ovens to micro-cassette recorders, from laptop word processors to laser disc players and digital video disc

Parker Pen U.S.A. Ltd.
1400 N Parker Dr., Jamesville, WI 53545, (608) 755-7000. Gift guide of pens that can be personalized with your company's logo or individual's name

PC Nametag
Topitzes & Assoc., 4200 University Ave., Ste. 2000, Madison, WI 53705, (608) 231-6109, FAX (800) 233-9787, Web site http://www. pcnametag.com Name tags

Pegi Goff Corporation
823 U.S. Highway 27 S., Lake Hamilton, FL

33851, (941) 439-5075. Manufactures cotton and fleece jerseys with animal appliqués and your company name and logo. Adult and children's sizes available

Physicians Sales & Service
7800 Belfort Pkwy., Ste. 250, Jacksonville, FL 32256, (904) 281-0011, FAX (904) 281-9555. Medical products distribution

Private Cellars Ltd.
2625 N. Chase Pkwy., Wilmington, NC 28405, (910) 791-1900. Can customize the labels on its bottles of champagne, packaged in gift boxes—wooden case or gift set with glasses

Private Eyes Sunglass Corporation
Barbara Winberg, 385 Fifth Ave., Ste. 902, New York, NY 10016, (212) 683-6663. Emmanuelle Kahn eye-wear, men's Gargoyles, Timberline, Hobie and Stussy eyewear, and a full line of eyewear accessories and repair kits

Promotional Products Unlimited
2301 W. 205th St., Suite 104, Torrance, CA 90501, (800) 748-6150. Offers huge selection of items incld. awards, plaques, pens, watches, golf balls and portfolios. All products can be customized

PSP Sports Marketing
Steve McKelvey, Custom Publishing Ser-vices, 355 Lexington Ave., New York, NY 10017, (212) 697-1460. Offers personalized desktop diary featuring profiles and color photos of America's Olympic heroes

Rand Ross
51 Executive Blvd., Farmingdale NY 11735, (516) 249 6000. Offers high quality bicycles and exercise equipment

REI (Recreational Equipment Inc.)
Commercial Sales Dept., P.O. Box 1700, Sumner, WA 98390, (800) 258-4567 or (253) 891-2523, FAX (206) 891-2523. Supply outdoor gear and clothing products and gift certificates

Royal Animated Art
20545 Plummer Street, Chatsworth, CA 92311, (800) 693-2369. Offers original production cells and hand-printed limited editions from animated films including Mighty Mouse, Heckel & Jeckel, Archie, Fat Albert, Flash Gordon and more

Santa's World Catalog
Kurt S. Adler Inc., 1107 Broadway, New York, NY 10010-2872, (800) 243-XMAS or (212) 924-0900. Features more than 20,000 Christmas items including Disney and Sesame Street characters

Seiko Corporation of America
The Premium Dept., 1111 MacArthur Blvd, Mahwah, NJ 07430, (800) 545-2783. Offers watches for color imprinting and embossed customization

Sentry
900 Linden Ave., Rochester, NY 14625, (800) 828-1438. Customized fire-safe products for protecting valuables

Sevylor U.S.A. Inc.
6651 E. 26th St., Los Angeles, CA 90040, (213) 727-6013. Full line of inflatable sports products like air mattresses, canoes, boats, and snow products

Sharp Electronics Corporation
J.P. Collins, Sharp Plaza, Mahwah, NJ 07430-2135, (201) 529-8638. Has a four-page incentive booklet with four tiers of gifts including boomboxes, audio-video systems, camcorders, microwave ovens and large-screen TVs

Skip Barber Racing School
(800) 221-1131. Offers classes in formula race-car driving at more than 20 different race tracks. They will arrange lodging, catering and professional photography

Smith & Hawken
117 E. Strawberry Dr., Mill Valley, CA 94941, (800) 776-3336 or (415) 383-4415. Garden catalogue

Sony Corporation
Park Ridge, NJ. (201) 930-1000. Offers electronic equipment that can be used for incentives

Specialty Graphics
4347 W. Northwest Hwy., Ste. 1010, Dallas, TX 75220, (800) 728-5490. The PIX Panorama camera can be imprinted with a company logo, and is priced at under $15

Sportcap
13401 S. Main St., Los Angeles, CA 90061, E-mail SPORTSCAP@AOL. COM Offers cotton caps screen-printed with a water sport or golf scene

Starbucks Coffee Co.
701 Fifth Ave., Seattle, WA 98104, (206) 447-9934. Coffee and related items

Stock Yards Packing Co.
Dan Rost, 340 N. Oakley Blvd., Chicago, IL 60612, FAX (312) 733-0738. Catalogue of gifts, such as steaks, seafood and gourmet treats

Subtle Media, Inc.
149 Lorenz, San Antonio, TX 78209, (800) 635-7261, FAX (210) 822-5959. Customizes a wide range of merchandise and office supplies

Sugardale's
Special Markets Division, P.O. Box 571, Dept. D, Massillon, OH 44648, (800) 860-5444. Offers 130 gourmet food items, such as whole smoked turkeys. They will include a personalized gift card

Swiss Army Brands, Inc.
1 Research Drive, P.O. Box 874, Shelton, CT 06484-0874, (800) 243-4066, FAX (800) 243-4025, Web site www.swissarmy.com Can custom imprint the Swiss Army Brand Watch and Swiss Army Knife

Telescope Casual Furniture, Inc.
Church Street, Granville, NY 12832, (518) 642-1100, ext. 272, Web site www. telescopecasual.com Offers umbrella, beach chairs and a full line of director chairs that can be customized with your company name and logo

Texas Instruments
Consumer Relations, P.O. Box 650311 M.S. 3962, Dallas, TX 75265, (800) TI-CARES, Web site www.ti.com Introducing their newest translator, the PS-5600 which can define 3,000 words. Translates English, German, French, Italian, Spanish and Dutch

Tiffany & Co.
727 Fifth Ave., New York, NY 10022, (212) 755-8000 or (800) 423-2394. Will custom engrave a sterling silver yo-yo, Swiss Army Knife, key chain, or other specialty item

Torrington Christine Photography
209 Post St., Ste. 812, San Francisco, CA 94108, (415) 921-6333, FAX (415) 986-3886. Professional photographers

Travel Graphics International
1118 S. Cedar Lake Rd., Minneapolis, MN 55405, (612) 377-1080, FAX (612) 377-1420. Graphics of promotional material for destination, pocket maps, posters

Tucker-Jones House
P.O. Box 231, E. Setauket, NY 11733, (516) 751-8960, Web site tavernpuzzle.com Metal puzzles offered. Packaging for puzzles can be personalized with company names and logos

Ultra Plateau Catalogs
(a division of KMart), Gift Certificate Administration, 3100 West Big Beaver Rd., Troy, MI 48084-3163, (800) 345-2497 or (313) 643-2560, FAX (313) 643-3207. Will custom imprint merchandise or apparel with your name, company name and/or logo.

Warner Books
Premium/Incentive Sales, 666 Fifth Ave., New York, NY 10103, (212) 522-5066 or (212) 484-3128. Customized books including Webster's Dictionary and Thesaurus

Waterford Wedgwood USA
Incentive Division, P.O. Box 1454, Wall, NJ 07719, (800) 933-3370 or (908) 938-5800. Features crystal and china at all price levels

Wells Lamont
6640 West Touhy Avenue, Niles, IL 60714, (800) 323-2830. Sells gloves that can be customized with your logo

Wilson Sporting Goods Co.
8700 W. Bryn Mawr Ave., Chicago, IL 60631, (800) 432-0321, Web site www. wilsonsport.com Will imprint a golf ball with your four-color logo or name. Also offers lazer-engraved putters and golf balls

Wittnauer International
Andrew Finn, Director of Sales, Special Markets, 145 Huguenot Street, New Rochelle, NY 10802, (800) 451-2242, Compuserve 73464,203compuserve. com Company no longer carries Longines products or any clocks. Just Wittnauer watch line and Zodiac watch line. Will customize products

Workman Publishing Co.
Special Markets Department, 708 Broadway, New York, NY 10003-9555 (212) 614-7509, E-mail andrea@workman.com Offers a full line of gift books, cookbooks, kids' books and calendars. Will create customized books and calendars (Page-A-Day® too) for corporate promotions and incentive programs

World Heritage Incentives
World Heritage Travel Group, Inc., 1211 Main St., Angels Camp, CA 95222, (800) 336-0933 or (209) 736-0933, FAX (209) 736-0333. Video production

Appendix II

Companies That Arrange Unusual Reward Activities

Adventure Connection
P.O. Box 475, Coloma, CA 95613, (800) 556-6060 or (916) 626-7385. River trips, whitewater rafting

Atlantis Submarine Adventure
dba Aruba Tourism Authority, 1 Financial Plaza #136, Fort Lauderdale, FL 33394, (954) 767-3395. Offers submarine tour of the waters off the Caribbean's only desert island, Aruba

Balloon Aviation
6525 Washington St., Ste. 7, Yountville, CA 94599-1300, (707) 252-7067, FAX (707) 944-0540. Hot air balloon tours

Balloons Above the Valley
5091 Solano Ave., Napa, CA 94558, (800) GO HOT AIR or (707) 464-6824. Hot-air balloon excursions

Black Canyon River Raft Tours
1297 Nevada Hwy, Boulder City, NV, (702) 293-3776. Group raft trips down the Colorado River

Boundry Country Trekking
590 Gunflint Trail, Grand Marais, MN 55604, (800) 322-8327. Offers cross-country ski trips in winter, guided canoe trips in summer, along with dog-sled trips

Brier and Dunn
2962 Filmore St., San Francisco, CA 94123, (415) 346-7801. Stages jungle theme dinners at the San Francisco Zoo

Burnside Marina
P.O. Box 577, Burnside, KY 42519, (606) 561-4223. Houseboat excursions

California Leisure Consultants
69730 Hwy. 111, Ste. 3109A, Rancho Mirage, CA 92270, (619) 324-5839, Web site www.pgi.com Offers unique theme events including: Indian-Western barbecues with stuntmen who stage a gunfight, or baseball games with players wearing vintage uniforms

Canadian Pacific Hotels and Resorts
360 N. Sepulveda, #2050, El Segundo, CA 90245, (310) 640-9959. A legendary 850-room castle in Banff Springs in the Canadian Rockies

Carlson Marketing Group
P.O. Box 59159, Carlson Parkway,

Minneapolis, MN 55459, (612) 540-5000, Web site www.carlsoncompaniesinc.com Houseboating and other excursions

Corporate Sports Incentives, Inc.
P.O. Box 578, Merrimack, NH 03054, (800) 633-5200 or (617) 229-2755, FAX (617) 229-8886. Golf and ski tickets

Deep Sea Charters
801 Seabreeze Blvd., Marina Tower, 2nd Fl., Fort Lauderdale, FL 33316, (954) 525-7724, Web site www.windridgeyachts.com Luxurious and elegant charter for corporate events or parties. 5-star-hotel dining quality

Echo Bay Resort
Overton, NV 89040, (702) 394-4000. Houseboating excursions

EGR International
271 Madison Avenue, New York, NY 10016, (800) 221-1072. Houseboating excursions

Family Living Rafting Guide
1231 N. Tustin Ave.,

Anaheim, CA 92807, (714) 632-9810. Rafting trips on rivers throughout the United States for families with children as young as four years old. Trips range from one-day getaways to multiweek adventures

Feather River Rail Society
P.O. Box 608, Portola, CA 96122, (916) 832-4131. Train fans and would-be engineers can go to the Portola Railroad Museum — the only place in the world where you can rent and drive a real locomotive. Railroad Museum also offers rides on cabooses and flatcars

Great American Treasure Hunt
654 Waller St., San Francisco, CA 94117, (415) 626-2950, FAX (415) 626-1445. Organizes teams on a treasure hunt through San Francisco via streetcars

Intourist
630 Fifth Ave., New York, NY 10020, (212) 757-3884. Holiday in Russia on a col-

lective farm including a visit to a recreational center for performances of folk music and dances

ITT Sheraton Corporation
60 State St., Boston, MA 02109, (617) 367-3600. Includes the Sheraton Parco de Medici, the first golf resort in Italy

Jamestown Resort and Marina
P.O. Box 530, Jamestown, KY 42629, (502) 343-5253. Houseboating excursions

La Costa Resort and Spa
Costa del Mar Road, Carlsbad, CA 92009, (800) 544-7483, Web site www.lacosta.com Offers a world-famous spa, golf courses, tennis courts and 300-seat night club

Mana, Allison & Associates
1388 Sutter St., #525, San Francisco, CA 94109, (415) 474-2266. Offers an array of leisure activities for conferences and conventions coming to San

Francisco, including Renaissance fairs.

Mandarin Singapore Hotel
dba Marina Mandarin Hotel, U.S. Sales Office, Joan Scheckter, 70-A Greenwich Ave., Ste. 316, New York, NY 10011, (212) 924-0882. Theme parties with ethnic food, Chinese orchestra, dancers and entertainers

Maritz Travel Company
1400 S. Highway Dr., Fenton, MO 63099, (314) 827-4848. Exclusively Yours Cheques, in denominations of $10 and $50 and redeemed for unique travel experiences including safaris, flying lessons, golf clinics and baseball camps

Marketing Innovators
9701 W. Higgins Road, Ste. 400, Rosemont, IL 60018, (847) 696-1111, Web site www. marketinginnovators. com Freedom to Choose® retail gift certificates

Marriott Hotels & Resorts
1 Marriott Dr.,

Washington, DC 20058, (301) 380-9000. Marriott Surfers Paradise Resort on Australia's Gold Coast features aquatic playground with beaches, lagoon, simulated coral reef and water sports

Memories Unlimited
4713 Larchmont Dr., Orlando, FL 32821, (407) 345-8922. Sports programs, children's events, theme activities

Micato Safaris
15 W. 26th St., New York, NY 10010, (800) 642-2861. Offers tented safari camps in Kenya and Tanzania

The Moorings
19345 U.S. Hwy., 19 N., Clearwater, FL 34624, (800) 437-7880 or (813) 530-5424, FAX (813) 530-9747. Yacht chartering company

Museum of Science and Industry
57th St. & Lake Shore Dr., Chicago, IL 60637, (800) 468-6674 or (312) 684-1414, FAX (312) 684-7141. Meeting facility

Mushing Magazine
P.O. Box 149, Ester, AI 99725, (907) 479-0454. Lists a number of companies offering dog-sledding trips

Napa Chamber of Commerce
1556 First Street, Napa, CA 94559-0636, (707) 226-7455. Complete list of companies that provide hot-air balloon excursions in the Napa Valley

Napa Valley Wine Train
1275 McKinstry St., Napa, CA 94559, (800) 427-2124 or (707) 253-2111, FAX (707) 253-9264. Scenic ride on 1915 Pullman train

Paragon Guides
P.O. Box 130, Vail, CO 81658, (970) 926-5299. Weekend or six-day backcountry hiking trips

A Party to Intrigue
654 Waller St., San Francisco, CA 94117, (415) 626-2950. Provides a murder mystery or treasure hunt especially for your group aboard the restored Napa Valley Wine Train

QuizMaster
dba Wizard, 8 Sojo Rd., Brookfield, CT 06810, (203) 740-7970. Offers customized corporate contests

Regent Sydney
Ron Posladek, Regent International Hotel, 199 George St., Sydney NSW 1220 AU, Australia, (800) 545-4000. Offers a camel safari and other exotic adventure packages

The Russian Tea Room
150 W. 57th St., New York, NY 10019, (800) 262-4787 or (212) 265-0947, FAX (212) 489-3968. Restaurant and cabaret

Safaris, Inc.
dba PGI Destination Management Business & Events Communications, 1202 Morena Blvd., Ste. 400, San Diego, CA 92110. Recreates the golden age of Hollywood for theme parties, including a theater marquee with your company name

Soaring Adventures of America, Inc.
P.O. Box 541, Wilton, CT 06897, (800)

762-7464. Sailplane and glider rides

Space Camp
Cannes, France, (011) 33-93-90-3618. Experience astronaut training camp

Star Clippers
4101 Salzedo, Coral Gables, FL 33146, E-mail stclipper@aol.com Groups sail on the world's only modern-day clipper ship

Sunrise Balloons
P.O. Box 891360 Temecula, CA 92589, (800) 548-9912, Web site www.sunrise.com Scenic balloon and helicopter tours and charters

10th Mountain Trail Association
1280 Ute Avenue, Aspen, CO 81611, (970) 925-5775, reservations, (970) 925-4554. Backcountry hiking trips

Vancouver Aquarium
Carole Rapp, Special Events Coordinator, P.O. Box 3232 Vancouver, B.C., Canada V6B 3X8, (604) 631-2502. Arranges activities, such as breakfast with beluga whales, cocktails with killer whales and

dinner among octopuses, sea otters, and other aquatic creatures for groups of up to 1,000

Venture-Up Mountain Expeditions
2415 E. Indian School Rd., Phoenix, AZ 85016, (602) 955-9100, Web site www.ventureup.com A corporate training and wilderness adventure company offers team-building courses. Newest location in Rawhide, North Scottsdale

Waterfall Resort
Mike Dooley, Reservations, P.O. Box 6440 Ketchikan, AK 99901, (800) 544-5125. Resort in Ketchikan, Alaska, offers mountain wildlife and salmon fishing. Also offers national wildlife trips and fly-fishing adventures

World Yacht
Pier 81, W. 41st & Hudson River, New York, NY 10036, (212) 630-8800, FAX (212) 630-8899, Web site www.worldyacht.com Yacht charters

Appendix III

Incentive Travel Coordinators

Activities, Inc.
53 Pennington-
Hopewell Rd.,
Pennington, NJ, (609)
466-4100 or (609)
466-5414

AM Incentive Travel
3 Fairbaim Rd., Kirkton
North, Livingston, W.L.
Scotland EH5 46TS,
(050) 646-0499, FAX
(050) 646-1211

Ann d'Eon Incentives
4515 S. McClintock Dr.,
Ste. 120, Tempe, AZ
85282, (602) 839-2225,
FAX (602) 839-0743

**Atlantis Submarine
Adventure**
dba Aruba Tourism
Authority,
1 Financial Plaza #136
Fort Lauderdale, FL
33394, (954) 767-3395

Atlas Motivation
201 Alhambra Circle,
Ste. 802, Coral Gables,
FL 33134

A.T.S. Pacific
40 Miller St., 3rd FL.,
North Sydney, Australia
2060, (612) 957-3811,
FAX (612) 957-1385

**Axis Sales and
Marketing**
18 Seymour Pl, London,
England W1H 5W H,
(471) 706-2220, FAX
(471) 706-2867

**Barberini Incentive-
Congressi SRL**
Barberini Tours SRL,
Via Sannio, 64, Rome,
Italy 00183, (314) 411-
3344, FAX (314) 556-
0788

Bateaux Parisiens
Sodexho Loisirs, Port
de la Bourdonais, Paris,
France 75007, (314)
411-3344, FAX (314)
556-0788

**Belgium International
Events**
Chassee D'ixelles 31,
Brussels, Belgium

B1050, (002) 513-3825,
FAX (002) 512-6918

Bell Tours, Inc.
12894 16th Ave.,
White Rock, B.C.,
Canada V4A 1N7,
(604) 536-8488, FAX
(604) 538-6646

Bixby Knolls Travel
5535 Stearns, Long
Beach, CA 90815,
E-mail
BKT200@AOL.COM

**Bonaventure
Incentives, Ltd.**
61 Rangitikei St.,
Palmerston North,
New Zealand, (006)
356-6102, FAX (006)
356-3230

**Canadian Pacific
Hotels and Resorts**
360 N. Sepulveda,
#2050, El Segundo, CA
90245, (310) 640-9959
or (212) 754-7800,

FAX (310) 640-9952, Web site http://www.cphotels.ca

Carlson Marketing Group
Carlson Companies, Inc., Level 5, 60 Albert Rd., S. Melbourne, Victoria, Australia, 3205, (613) 690-1200, FAX (613) 699-6859

Carlson Tours & Incentive Travel Ltd.
4646 Riverside Dr., Ste. 14A, Red Deer, Alta., Canada T4N 6Y5

Carrousel Yacht
1717 N. Bayshore Dr., Ste. 2500, Miami, FL 33138, (800) 950-5336 or (305) 530-9700, FAX (305) 377-3297

Classic Cruise & Travel Co.
19720 Ventura Blvd., Ste. A, Woodland Hills, CA 91364, (818) 346-8747, FAX (818) 346-1492

Convention Consultants
117 W. Perry St., Savannah, GA 31401, (912) 233-4088

CPO Hanser Service
Zum Ehrenhain 34, Hanburg-Barsbuttel, Germany 2000,

(040) 670-6051, FAX (040) 670-3283

Creative Group Inc.
619 N. Lyndale Dr., Appleton, WI 54914-3022, (920) 739-8850, FAX (920) 739-8817

Creative Incentives
Creative Travel Consultants, Inc., 4225 Baltimore, Kansas City, MO 64111-2322, (800) 821-7674 or (816) 753-7651, FAX (816) 753-7877, Web site http://creativeincentives.com

Creative Travel Planners, Inc.
5855 Topanga Canyon Blvd., Ste. 220, Woodland Hills, CA 91367, (800) 255-3070 or (818) 704-7033, FAX (818) 347-4113

Curaçao Chamber of Commerce and Industry
Kaya Junior Salas #1, P.O. Box 10, Willemstad, Curaçao, N.A. 611451, (599) 961-1451, FAX (599) 961-5652

Destination Management
Kowkoeklaan 140, Bussum, Netherlands 1403 EK

The Destination Manager & Business Incentives
Sanadiki Travel, P.O. Box 7784-Argentine St., Damascus, Syria, (963) 11239800, FAX (963) 11243503

Destination Marketing Group, Inc.
Karin Nelson, P.O. Box 71, Wayzata, MN 55391, (800) 739-9331, E-mail BHARRIS@SKYPOINT.COM; Web site www.destinationsa-b.com

Destination Services, Unique Locations
255 N. El Cielo, Ste. 252, Palm Springs, CA 92262, (619) 322-0243, FAX (619) 327-5599, E-mail julierupp@earthlink.net

Diethelm Travel
Diethelm & Co., Ltd., Kian Gwan Bldg. 11, 140-1 Wireless Rd., Bangkok, Thailand 10330, (662) 255-9150, FAX (662) 254-9018

Dilon Enterprises Intl.
163 Third Ave., Ste. 147, New York, NY 10003, (212) 953-4010, FAX (212) 260-5538

Diners Fugzy Travel
105 W. Adams St.,

Chicago, IL 60603,
(312) 263-4212

**Discount Hotel
Rates–Zatman
Marketing**
165 8th Street, Ste.
201, San Francisco, CA
94103, (800) 423-7846
or (415) 252-1107

**Dittman Incentive
Marketing Corp.**
2015 Lincoln Hwy.,
Edison, NJ 08817,
(908) 248-0707

**EGR International
Meetings & Incentives**
271 Madison Ave., New
York, NY 10016, (212)
949-7330

Excellence Ltd.
Artillery Row, 50
Westminster Palace
Gardens, London,
England SW1P 1RR,
(071) 222-9451, FAX
(071) 799-2215

**Extra Mile Company
(Pty.), Ltd.**
P.O. Box 707, Lonehill,
Johannesburg, South
Africa 2062

Famous Events Groups
504-68 Water St., Van-
couver, B.C., Canada
V6B 1A4, (604) 689-
3448, FAX (604) 689-
5245

Feldman Associates
505 N. Lakeshore Dr.,
Ste. 6601, Chicago, IL
60611, Web site
www.itcheque.com

**Paul Foster Travel &
Tours**
Foster & Inc. Ltd., dba
Foster & Ince Cruise
Services, Inc. Erin
Court, Bishop's Court
Hill, Collymore Rock,
Saint Michael, Barba-
dos, (246) 431-8946

**Frazier & Hoyt
Incentives**
Frazier & Hoyt Grp.,
1801 Hollis St., Ste.
1010, Halifax, NS,
Canada B3J3N4, (902)
421-1113, FAX (902)
425-3756, Web site
www.frazierhoyt.com

**Frontier Travel
Incentives, Inc.**
2620 S. Parker Rd.,
Ste. 105, Aurora, CO
80014, (303) 368-7676
or (303) 671-6502,
E-mail FRONTIER@
EZ.NET

**GB Internacional
Transporte e
Turismo Ltda.**
Rua Capitao Salomao
40, Rio de Janeiro,
Brazil 22271-040,
(521) 286-9697, FAX
(521) 286-9484

**Graham Marketing
Group**
980 Loan Oak Rd., Ste.
114, Eagan, MN 55121

**Greater Lansing
Convention & Visitors
Bureau**
P.O. Box 15066, 119
Pere Marquette,
Lansing, MI 48901-
5066, (800) 648-6630
or (517) 487-0007,
FAX (517) 487-5151,
Web site
www.lansing.org

**The Greater
Sherbrooke Tourist
Development Corp.**
1308 Portland Blvd.,
C.P. 426, Sherbrooke,
PQ, Canada J1H5J7,
(819) 822-6195, FAX
(819) 822-6074

The Hart Line
165 Aldershot Ln.,
Manhasset, NY 11030,
(516) 627-7725

**The Helin
Organization**
1 Corporate Plaza, Ste.
100, Newport Beach,
CA 92660, (800) 325-
7103, (714) 717-5050,
FAX (714) 717-5051

Holiday Models Corp.
Convention Services
900 E. Desert Inn Rd.
Ste. 101, Las Vegas,
NV 89109,

(702) 735-7353, FAX
(702) 796-5676

Holt Paris Welcome Service
12 Rue du Helder,
Paris, France 75009,
(452) 308-14, FAX
(474) 919-89

Hotels of Switzerland
104 S. Michigan Ave.,
Ste. 802, Chicago, IL
60603, (312) 782-1912,
FAX (312) 782-0143,
Web site
www.swissplan.com

Human Motivation Pty. Ltd.
P.O. Box 820, Arta-
mon, Australia NSW
2064, (002) 906-6222,
FAX (002) 906-6110

Incentivar - Contactos Ltda.
Av. San Martin Centro
Comercial Bocagrande
20., Piso Local 216
Boca-grande/Cartagena
C/BIA, Cartagena,
Columbia, (654) 559-
6061, FAX (575) 365-
2327

Incentive Holland Business Events bv
P.O. Box 460, 3430 AL
Nieuwegein, The
Netherlands, 31-30-
604 2545, FAX 31-30-
604 3094,
E-mail incentv@

worldaccess.nl; Web
site www.incentive.nl

Incentive Solutions
2136 Westlake N,
Seattle, WA 98109,
(206) 283-7176 FAX
(206) 283-5508

Incentive Strategies
dba Cornerstone
86 Pleasant St., Marl-
boro, MA 01752, (800)
825-5494 or (508)
460-1900, FAX (508)
460-9996

Incentive Travelers Cheque, Inc.
505 N. Lakeshore Dr.,
Ste. 6601, Chicago, IL
60611, (312) 280-1988,
Web site
www.itcheque.com

INCOMA/Incentive Congress & Marketing Service
Nieder-Roeder-Weg
12, Heusenstamm,
Germany DW-6056,
(061) 046-5024, FAX
(061) 046-7774

Intermedia Convention & Event Management
Intermedia House,
P.O. Box 1280, Milton
Qld., Australia 4064,
(617) 369-0477, FAX
(617) 369-1512

International Meeting Planners
18662 MacArthur Blvd.,
Ste. 200, Newport
Beach, CA 92715,
(714) 252-9250, FAX
(714) 955-1104

International Travel Associates Group
4800 Westown Pkwy.,
Regency West 3, West
Des Moines, IA 50266,
(800) 257-1985 or
(515) 224-3400, FAX
(515) 224-3552, Web
site www.itagroup.com

International Travel Incentives, Inc.
1921 E. Carnegie Ave.,
Ste. 3H, Santa Ana, CA
92705, (714) 757-0490,
FAX (714) 757-0926

Intourist
630 Fifth Ave., New
York, NY 10020, (212)
757-3884

ITT Sheraton Corporation
60 State St., Boston,
MA 02109, (617) 367-
3600

Jecking Tours & Travel, Ltd.
7th Fl. China Insurance
Bldg., 48 Cameron Rd.,
Kowloon, Hong Kong,
(852) 739-1188, FAX
(852) 721-2748

JNR Inc.
2603 Main St., 2nd Fl.,
Irvine, CA 92614

The Journeymasters, Inc.
254 Essex St., Salem,
MA 01970, (800) 875-
3422 or (508) 745-
4500, FAX (508)
741-4816, Web site
www.journeymasters@
aol.com

Kirby Tours
2451 S. Telegraph,
Dearborn, MI 48124,
(800) 521-0711 or
(313) 278-2224, FAX
(313) 278-9569, E-mail
kirby@kirbytours.com;
Web site
www.kirbytours.com

Krebs Convention Management Services
555 De Haro St., Ste.
333, San Francisco, CA
94107-2348, (415)
255-1295, FAX (415)
255-2244, E-mail
krebsconv@aol.com;
Web site
www.citysearch.com/
sfo/krebs

Kuoni Travel Ltd.
7 rue de Berne CH
1201, Geneva,
Switzerland
(+41 22) 908-18-11,
FAX (+41 22) 731-50-
78

Kuban Tours
1061 Rue Liege W.,
Montreal, PQ, Canada
H3N 2B9, (514) 274-
2692, FAX (514) 274-
3140

Kushner & Associates
Custom Tours, Inc.
1104 S. Robertson
Blvd., Los Angeles, CA
90035, (310) 274-8819,
FAX (310) 273-9535,
E-mail
califdmc@aol.com

Kustom Incentive Concepts, Inc.
31877 Del Obispo, Ste.
106 A, San Juan
Capistrano, CA 92675,
(714) 493-1050, FAX
(714) 493-1214

Landry & Kling Cruise Specialists
1390 S. Dixie Hwy.,
Ste. 1207, Coral
Gables, FL 33146,
(800) 448-9002 or
(305) 661-1880, FAX
(305) 661-0977

Leaders in Travel
200 Middleneck Rd.,
Great Neck, NY
11021-1103, (800)
327-5947 or (516)
829-0880, FAX (516)
829-0895

Light Group, Inc.
424 Madison Ave.,
New York, NY 10017,

(212) 486-4300, FAX
(212) 755-2135, E-mail
mincentive2@aol.com;
Web site
www.wbs.com/light

Gerry Lou & Associates
1224 Stanley St., Ste.
311, Montreal, PQ,
Canada H3B 2S7, (514)
878-2530, FAX (514)
878-2532

Longue Vue House & Gardens
7 Bamboo Rd., New
Orleans, LA 70124,
(504) 488-5488 FAX
(504) 486-7015,
Web site
www.longuevue.com

Mandarin Oriental Hotel Group
11835 West Olympic,
Ste. 775, Los Angeles,
CA 90064, (310) 479-
0570

Maren & Associates
899 Skikie Blvd., Ste.
420, Northbrook, IL
60062, (887) 564-2400,
FAX (887) 564-2539

Mariner Hotel Corporation
dba Remmington Hotel
Group, 14180 Dallas
Pkwy., 9th Fl., Dallas,
TX 75240, (972) 980-
2700, FAX (972) 980-
2705

Marriott Hotels & Resorts
Marriott Drive, Washington, DC 20058, (301) 380-9000, Web site www.marriott.com

MICA (Meetings, Incentives, Conventions of America)
34 Jerome Ave., Bloomfield, CT 06002, (800) 275-6422, (860) 286-8900, FAX (860) 726-1986, E-mail pluby@ internationaltravel.com

Monark Turismo
Rua Dom Jose Gaspar 134-10, A, Sao Paulo, Brazil 0107-900

Helen Moskovitz & Assocs.
95 White Bridge Rd., Ste. 500, Nashville, TN 37205, (615) 352-6900, Web site www. helenmoskovitz.com

Motiv Action
9800 Sheland Pkwy., Minneapolis, MN 55441, (800) 326-2226, (612) 544-7200, Web site www.motivaction.com

Motivation
Avenue de Lavaux 101, Pully, Switzerland 1009, (412) 129-9754, FAX (412) 129-9758

Mount Snow Vermont Tours
dba New England Vacation Tours P.O. Box 560, Rt. 100, West Dover, VT 05356-0560, (800) 742-7669 or (802) 464-2076, FAX (802) 464-2629

Newtours Travel Agency
Via Guido. Monaco 20, 50144 Florence, Italy, (039) 55 322011, FAX (039) 55 3220110

Newtours & CMO
Via S. Donato 20-22 50122 Florence, Italy, (039) 55 33611, FAX (039) 55 3361250/350

Norwegian Cruise Line
7665 Corporate Center Dr., Miami, FL 33126, (305) 436-4000, FAX (305) 436-4111

Ocean Concepts
3415 Sepulveda Blvd., Ste. 645, Los Angeles, CA 90034, (800) 442-7222 or (310) 397-7499

Olsen O'Leary Travel Inc.
565 Epsilon Dr., Pittsburgh, PA 15238, (412) 963-7272, FAX (412) 963-9773

Orange County Convention Center
9800 International Dr., Orlando, FL 32819, (800) 345-9845 or (407) 345-9800, FAX (407) 345-9876, E-mail http:// www. citizens-first.co. orange.sl.us

P & L International Vacationers
One Sherwood Street, Picadilly Circus, London, England WIV 7RA, (071) 437-9915, FAX (071) 437-7124

Panorama Destination Management Co.
P.O. Box 4544, Rua Dr. Joao Brito Camara 3-AVB, Funcal, Portugal, (351) 912-91945, FAX (351) 912-8312

Paragon Guides
P.O. Box 130, Vail, CO 81658, (970) 926-5299

Passport Tour Company
P.O. Box 816, North Sydney, NSW, Australia

2060, (612) 957-2700, FAX (612) 957-1478

PEP Enterprises
7325 N. 16th St., Ste. 100, Phoenix, AZ 85020, (602) 944-2080, FAX (602) 944-2188

Port Ludlow Golf and Meeting Retreat
200 Olympic Pl., Ludlow, WA 98365, (800) 732-1239, E-mail portludlow@ olympus.net

Professional Meeting Organizers, Inc.
9966 S.W. 26th St., Miami, FL 33165-2636, (305) 221-3922

Professional Touch
2 Oak Way, Berkeley Heights, NJ 07922, (800) 631-7373 or (908) 790-0100, FAX (908) 790-0173

Queensland Creative Destinations
P.O. Box 7068, Gold Coast Mail Centre, Gold Coast, Queensland, Australia 4217, (617) 592-3655, FAX (617) 531-6604

Regent Sydney
Ron Posladek, Regent International Hotel, 119 George St., Sydney, NSW 2000,

Australia, (800) 545-4000

Resort Marketing Associates, Inc.
3957 Holcomb Bridge Rd., #200, Norcross, GA 30092, (770) 662-5331

Riser/Almeida Associates, Inc.
Events Management 250 Montgomery St., 6th Fl., San Francisco, CA 94104, (415) 391-1446, FAX (415) 391-5407, E-mail raevents @travel.tfair.com

Robert Black Consultants
237 Park Ave., Ste. 2100, New York, NY 10017-3142, (212) 551-1437, FAX (212) 697-8486

Rogal Associates, Inc.
dba McGettigan Partners, Rogal Division, 70 Langley Rd., Newton Centre, MA 02159, (617) 965-1000, Web site http://www. mcgettigan.com

S & H Motivation
5999 Butterfield Rd., Hillside, IL 60162, (708) 449-4900, FAX (708) 449-4935

Shree Ram Enterprises, Inc.
Hampton Inn, 1-95 & Hwy. 204, 17007 Abercon St., Savannah, GA 31419, (800) 426-7866 or (912) 925-1212, FAX (912) 925-1227

Silkway Travel Ltd.
15-F, Kaiseng Commercial Ctr., 4-6 Hawkow Rd., Hong Kong, Hong Kong, (011) 724-0888, FAX (011) 721-7640

Sino-American Tours
37 Bowery St., New York, NY 10002, (212) 966-5866, FAX (212) 925-6483, E-mail sinotours@ix. netcom.com

Sita World Travel (India) Pvt., Ltd.
Inbound Tours, Dept. 4, Malcha Marg Shopping Centre, Diplomatic Enclave, New Delhi, India 110021, (911) 301-1122, FAX (911) 301-0123

Sitework Associates, Inc.
P.O. Box 158, Lambert, NJ 08530, (215) 794-2700, E-mail sitework@ worldnet.att.net

Smith, Bucklin & Associates, Inc.
401 N. Michigan Ave., Chicago, IL 60611-4267, (312) 644-6610, FAX (312) 321-6869

Smith Design Associates
P.O. Box 190, 205 Thomas St., Glen Ridge, NJ 07028 or (201) 429-2177, FAX (201) 429-2119, E-mail assoc @smithdesign.com

Space Camp
Cannes, France, (011) 33-93-90-3618

The Special Events Group, Inc.
245 E. 54th St., Ste. 24A, New York, NY 10022, (212) 319-9145, FAX (212) 319-8674

Spectacular Sport Specials
5813 Citrus Blvd., New Orleans, LA 70123-5810, (800) 451-5772 or (504) 734-9511, FAX (504) 734-7075, E-mail sportjab@ ix.netcom.com

Star Clippers
4101 Salzedo St., Coral Gables, FL 33146, (800) 442-0551

State of Tennessee Department of Tourist Development
320 6th Ave., 5th fl., Nashville, TN 37243, (615) 741-2159, Web site http://www. state.tn.us/tourdev/

Successful Incentive Travel
Allied World Travel, 899 Skokie Blvd., Northbrook, IL 60062, (800) 323-8268, (708) 272-9010, FAX (708) 272-8214

Sunbelt Motivation & Travel, Inc.
909 E. Las Colinas Blvd., Ste. 200, Irving, TX 75039, (214) 401-0210, FAX (214) 556-0916

Sunquest Incentive Travel
130 Merton St., Toronto, Ont., Canada M4S 1A4, (416) 485-1700, FAX (416) 485-6506

10th Mountain Trail Association
1280 Ute Avenue, Aspen, CO 81611, (970) 925-4554, reservations (970) 925-5775

Tirol Special Events & Tours
Joe Travel Touristic,

Seefeld, Austria 6100, (435) 212-3813, FAX (435) 212-4915

Tours De Force Events
dba Empire Force Events, 71 W. 23rd St., Ste. 1610, New York, NY 10010, (212) 924-0320, FAX (212) 675-9106

Tourservice Gmbh
Aulgasse 176, Siegburg, Germany D-5200, (022) 416-2031, FAX (022) 415-5669

Transeair Travel, Inc.
2813 McKinley Pl. NW, Washington, DC 20015, (202) 362-6100, FAX (202) 362-7411

Travel and Transport Inc.
601 Locust St., Ste. 101, Des Moines, IA 50309, (800) 373-5083 or (515) 243-5083, FAX (515) 243-5517

Travelcorp
7401 Metro Blvd., Ste. 350, Minneapolis, MN 55439, (612) 831-8300, FAX (612) 831-7071, Web site www.travelcorp.com

Travel Dimensions, Ltd.
P.O. Box 36114, Northcote, Auckland,

New Zealand NIL, (649) 480-5862, FAX (649) 480-1145

Travel Inc.
3680 N. Peachtree Rd., Atlanta, GA 30341-2390, (770) 455-6575, FAX (770) 452-2712

Travel Incentives Limited
12-14 Penn Place, Rickmansworth, Herts, England WD3 1RE

Travel New Orleans, Inc.
400 Magazine St., Ste. 201, New Orleans, LA 70130, (800) 535-8747 or (504) 561-8747, FAX (504) 565-3550, Web site http://www.travelneworleans.com

Travelmore/Carlson Travel Network
1723 South Bend Ave., South Bend, IN 46637, (219) 271-4880

Turytravel
Viamonte 524, 3rd Fl., Buenos Aires, Argentina 1053, (541) 311-1480, FAX; (541) 319-8674

Universal Marketing & Incentives
World Travel Partners Co., 201 N. Unim St., Ste. 350, Alexandria,

VA 22314, (800) 772-9501, (703) 549-2769

USA Hosts
1055 E. Tropicana, Ste. 625, Las Vegas, NV 89119, (800) 634-6133 or (702) 798-0000, FAX (702) 798-5396

US Motivation
US Travel, 3379 Peachtree Rd. N.E., Atlanta, GA 30326, (404) 261-1600, FAX (404) 266-1729

United Incentives Inc.
150 N. 2nd St., Philadelphia, PA 19106, (215) 625-2700, FAX (215) 625-2502

United Touring International (U.S.A.), Inc.
dba United Touring Company, International Tours, African Tours, 1 Bala Plaza, Ste. 414, Bala Cynwyd, PA 19004, (800) 223-6486 or (610) 617-3300, FAX (610) 617-3312

Vantage Adventures
1324 E. North St. , Greenville, SC 29605, (803) 233-7703, FAX (803) 233-3864

Vantage Marketing Inc.
Eagle Intl. Corp., P.O. Box 39446, Minneapolis, MN 55439, (612) 941-5306, FAX (612) 941-6356

Virginia Escape Ltd.
215 McLaws Cir., Ste. 1, Williamsburg, VA 23185, (757) 229-1161, FAX (757) 229-4207, E-mail vaescapdmc@ aol.com

Vista Travel, Inc.
1 Kendall Square Building 700, Cambridge, MA 02139, (617) 621-0100, FAX (617) 621-0101

Walther's Tours Pty. Ltd.
P.O. Box 3247, Randburg, South Africa, 2125, (271) 789-3624, FAX (271) 789-5255

Waterfall Resort
Chick Baird, 1170 Coast Village Rd., Ste. 211, Santa Barbara, CA 93108, (805) 969-8780 or (805) 969-8783, E-mail wciwest@ msn.com; Web site www.wciinc.com

Wilkintours Limited
Corrie House, 48-54 London Rd., Staines;

London, England TW
184JB

Wilshire James
Meetings and Events,
Level 18, AMP Centre,
50 Bridge St., Sydney,
Australia 20000, (022)
011-400, FAX (022)
011-422

**World Class
Incentives**
2560 Ninth St.,
Berkeley, CA 94710,
(510) 486-0990, FAX
(510) 486-1010, E-mail
waterfal@ktn.com;
Web site
www.aipr.com

**World Heritage
Incentives**
World Heritage Travel
Goup, Inc., 1211 Main
St., Angels Camp, CA
95222, (800) 336-0930
or (209) 736-0933,
FAX (209) 736-0333

World Incentives
World Travel Agency,
13th Fl., African Life
Centre, 111
Commissioneri,
Johannesburg, South
Africa, (001) 129-7234,
FAX (001) 337-9485

Appendix IV

Motivational and Incentive Companies and Associations

Adcentive Group, Inc.
6675 Convoy Court, San Diego, CA 92111, (619) 278-9200. Unique employee recognition and motivational programs

American Rental Assoc.
1900 19th St., Moline, IL 61265, (800) 334-2177 or (309) 764-2475, FAX (309) 764-1533. Trade association

Association of Retail Marketing Services, Inc.
3 Caro Ct., Red Bank, NJ 07701-2315, (908) 842-5070. Trade association

Business Incentives
dba B.I. Performance 7630 Bush Lake Rd., Edina, MN 55439, (612) 835-4800. Incentive consulting company

Edward Enterprises, Inc.
641 Waiakamilo Rd., Honolulu, HI 96817, (808) 841-4231, FAX (808) 841-7707. Convention printing, newsletters, programs

Extraordinary Events
2457A South Hiawassee Rd., Ste. 120, Orlando, FL (407) 897-3933, FAX (407) 894-4446

Famous Events Group
dba Famous Events Group Destinations 504-68 Water St., Vancouver, B.C., Canada, V6B 1A4, (604) 689-3448, FAX (604) 689-5245. Supplier of theme decor, entertainment and corporate events

The Golf Card
164 Inverness Dr., E., Inglewood, CO 80155, (800) 321-8269. Golf discount card

Graham Marketing Group, Inc.
980 Lone Oak Rd., Ste. 114, Eagan, MN 55121, (612) 681-0055, FAX (612) 681-9261. Trade show management services

The Greater Sherbrooke Tourist Development Corp. .
1308 Portland Blvd., C.P. 426, Sherbrooke, PQ, Canada J1H5J7, (819) 822-6195, FAX (819) 822-6074. Trade association

Incentive Magazine
355 Park Ave. South, New York, NY 10010, (212) 592-6200. Magazine

Intermedia Convention & Event Management
Intermedia House,

P.O. Box 1280, Milton, Queensland, Australia 4064, (617) 369-0477, FAX (617) 369-1512. Conference organizers

International Exhibitors Assn.
5501 Backlick Rd., Ste. 200, Springfield, VA 22151, (703) 941-3725, FAX (703) 941-8275. Trade association

Cato Johnson
1 South Wacker Dr., Ste. 2000, Chicago, IL 60606, (312) 634-0200. Promotions agency

Kohala Coast Resort
H002 Box 5300, Kohala, HI 96743-5000, (808) 885-4915, FAX (808) 885-1044. Resort association

KVL Audio Visual Services, Inc.
6 Executive Plaza, Yonkers, NY 10701, (800) 862-3210 or (914) 965-8300, FAX (914) 965-8404. Event staging, video production

Howard Lanin Productions, Inc.
59 E. 54th St., New York, NY 10022, (212) 752-0960, FAX (212) 752-7065

London Entertains
Rank Organization, 1 Thameside Centre, Ken Bridge Rd., Brentford, Middlesex, England TW8 OHF. Restaurants and conference facilities

Mana, Allison and Associates
1388 Sutter St., #525, San Francisco, CA 94109, (415) 474-226-6249. Motivational consultants

Marden Kane Inc.
410 Lakeville Rd., Lake Success, NY 11042, (516) 326-3666. Promotional firm

Maritz Motivation Co.
1375 N. Hwy. Dr., Fenton, MO 63099, (314) 827-4000. Motivational consulting

Marketing Innovators
9701 W. Higgins Rd., Rosemont, IL 60018, (847) 696-1111, Web site marketing innovators.com Freedom to Choose® retail gift certificates

Media Systems, Inc.
727 Wainee St., Ste. 201, Lahaina, HI 96761, (800) 398-2271 or (808) 667-2271.

Computer graphic production

Mount Snow Vermont Tours
dba New England Vacation Tours P.O. Box 560, Rt. 100, West Dover, VT 05356-0560, (800) 742-7669 or (802) 464-2976, FAX (802) 464-2629. Independent meeting planners

Roy Moody & Associates
Albuquerque, NM, (505) 344-8390. Leadership and motivational seminars

Motivational Systems
395 Pleasant Valley, West Orange, NJ 07052, (201) 669-3777. Motivational consulting firm

National 4-H Center
Natl. 4-H Council, 7100 Connecticut Ave., Chevy Chase, MD 20815-4999, (301) 961-2840, FAX (301) 961-2894. Trade association

Orange County Convention Center
9800 International Dr., Orlando, FL 32819, (800) 345-9845 or (407) 345-9800,

FAX (407) 345-9876. Convention facility

Playfair
2207 Oregon St., Berkeley, CA 94705, (510) 540-8768. Humor and motivational consultants

Robert Black Consultants
237 Park Ave., Ste. 2100, New York, NY 10017-3142.

Sitework Associates, Inc.
P.O. Box 158, Lambertville, NJ 08530, (800) 323-1927 or (215) 794-2700, FAX (215) 794-2704. Conference site finding services

Smith, Bucklin & Assoc. Inc.
401 N. Michigan Ave., Chicago, IL 60611-4267, (312) 644-6610, FAX (312) 321-6869. Printing

Society of Incentive Travel
21 W. 38th St., 10th Fl., New York, NY 10018-5584, (212) 575-0910, FAX (212) 575-1838. Travel incentive information, promotional and research society

Star-Seigle McCombs
1001 Bishop St., Pacific Tower 19th FL, Honolulu, HI 96813, (808) 524-5080, FAX (808) 523-7443. Advertising for group conventions

Xerox Corp.
Xerox Business Services, 200 Madison Ave., New York, NY 10016, (212) 561-6700, FAX (212) 686-8224. Rental of copiers and business equipment

Appendix V

Featured Companies

Acapulco Restaurants,
p. 93
Long Beach, CA.
Food service

ACCO International,
p. 136
Deerfield, IL.
Manufactures office
products and supplies

**Action Management
Associates,** *p. 108*
Dallas, TX.
Training company

**Advanced Micro
Devices,** *pp. 78, 129,
148*
Sunnyvale, CA.
Manufactures and
markets complex
monolithic circuits

Advanta Corporation,
pp. 20, 76, 124, 198
Horsham, PA.
Financial services

Aerospatiale, *p. 81*
Paris, France.
Airplane, satellite and
missile manufacture

AFL-CIO, *p. 216*
(American Federation
of Labor-Congress of
Industrial Organiza-
tions), Washington,
D.C.
Union organization

Air Force, U.S.,
pp. 150, 195
Arlington, VA.
Military

Air France, *p. 34–35*
New York, NY.
Airline

**American Academy of
Ophthalmology,**
p. 182
San Francisco, CA.
Educational services

American Airlines,
p. 107
Dallas, TX.
Airline

American Express,
pp. 55, 100–1
New York, NY.
Financial Services,
magazines, information
services

**American General
Life,** *p. 30*
Nashville, TN.
Life and casualty
insurance

**American Honda
Motor Company,**
p. 130
Torrance, CA.
Automobile sales and
service

**American Hospital
Association,** *p. 121*
Chicago, IL.
Health care

**American President
Lines,** *p. 15–18*
Oakland, CA.
Transportation and
real estate

**American Savings
Bank,** *p. 114*
Irvine, CA.
Savings and loan

**American Society
on Aging,** *p. 54*
San Francisco, CA.
Services for and
research on needs of
the aging

Bell Labs, *p. 194*
Murray Hill, NJ.
Research and development division of AT&T

Ben and Jerry's, *p. 214*
Waterbury, VT.
Makes and distributes ice cream

Beneficial Management Corporation of America, *p. 211*
Peapack, NJ.
Provides management services

Black & Decker Corporation, *pp. 83, 108–9*
Towson, MD.
Power tools, appliances, hardware

Blanchard Training and Development, *pp. 25, 31, 70, 77, 82, 127, 191, 206*
Escondido, CA.
Management training products and services

Blue Cross/Blue Shield Association, *pp. 91, 174*
Chicago, IL.
Health insurers

Boise Cascade, *p. 136*
Boise, ID.
Paper, building and office products

Brasseler USA, *p. 190*
Savannah, GA.

Retailer for drill bits for dentists

Brunswick Mining and Smelting Corporation, *p. 105*
Bathurst, New Brunswick, Canada.
Mining company

Burger King, *pp. 50, 193*
Miami, FL.
Fast food restaurant chain

Busch Gardens, *pp. 5, 13*
Tampa, FL.
Entertainment

Busch Stadium, *p. 121–22*
St. Louis, MO.
Sports stadium

Cal Snap & Tab, *p. 149–50*
City of Industry, CA.
Produces business forms

Canon USA, *p. 59*
Lake Success, NY.
Marketing and distribution of printers and copiers

CareerTrack, *p. 43*
Boulder, CO.
Management seminars

Carillon Importers, *p. 34–35*
Teaneck, NJ.

Importers of Absolut vodka and other liquors

Carlson Marketing Group, *pp. 26, 63, 132*
Minneapolis, MN.
Trading stamp, coupon redemption; manufactures and distributes telescopes and binoculars

Cathay Pacific Airways Limited, *p. 62*
Los Angeles, CA.
Transportation services

Celestial Seasonings, Inc., *p. 49*
Boulder, CO.
Herbal tea company

Cellular One, *p. 123*
Indianapolis, IN.
Telephone communications

Central Bank of the South, *p. 82–83*
Birmingham, AL.
Financial services

Central Telephone Company of Illinois, *p. 68–69*
Des Plaines, IL.
Telephone utility

Ceramics Process Systems Corporation, *p. 95–96*
Milford, MA.
Technical ceramics manufacturer

Copley Memorial Hospital, p. 152
Aurora, IL.
Medical services

Coronet/MTI Film and Video, p. 127
Deerfield, IL.
Production and distribution of educational films

Covenant House, pp. 35, 142
New York, NY.
Social services

Cumberland Farms, p. 193
Canton, MA.
Convenience stores

Cuno, p. 177–78
Meriden, CT.
Manufactures water filtration and purification systems

Cyanamid Canada, p. 108
Winnipeg, Manitoba, Canada.
Pharmaceutical company

Cygna Group, p. 43
Oakland, CA.
Engineering and consulting

D'Agostino's, pp. 38, 91, 201–2
New Rochelle, NY.
Supermarket chain

Dairy Mart, pp. 84, 161
Enfield, CT.
Convenience stores

Dallas, TX, p. 220
Local government

Dana Corporation, pp. 36, 204
Toledo, OH.
Manufactures and distributes components for truck and industrial vehicles

Dan River Company, p. 203
Danville, VA.
Textile mill

D.D.B. Needham Worldwide, pp. 65, 224
New York, NY.
Advertising agency

Decatur, IL, p. 68
Local government

Delta Airlines, pp. 65, 117, 215, 220
Atlanta, GA.
Transportation services

Delta Business Systems, p. 49–50
Orlando, FL.
Sells business machines

Denny's, p. 119
Spartanburg, SC.
Restaurant chain

Diamond Fiber Products, p. 167–68
Thorndike, MA.
Manufactures egg cartons

Digital Equipment Corporation, pp. 75–76, 183
Maynard, NY.
Computers, software, peripherals

The Walt Disney Company, pp. 27, 43, 191, 194, 209
Burbank, CA.
Theme parks and resorts, consumer products, movie production

Dr. Pepper/Seven-Up Companies, Inc., p. 187–88
Dallas, TX.
Soft drink manufacturer

Domino's Pizza Distribution Company, pp. 77, 176
Ann Arbor, MI.
Fast food chain

Donnelly Mirrors, p. 204
Holland, MI.
Mirrors, windows and other glass products

Dow Chemical Company, *p. 73*
Midland, MI.
Chemical products, plastic products, consumer products

E. I. du Pont de Nemours and Company, *pp. 55, 189*
Wilmington, DE.
Energy, consumer products, insecticides, firearms, pharmaceuticals, industrial chemicals, medical products

Eastman Kodak Company, *pp. 32–33, 78, 109*
Rochester, NY.
Photographic products and services, chemicals, imaging, information services

Electro Scientific Industries, *p. 36*
Erie, PA.
Laser trimming devices and testing equipment used by electronics manufacturers

Elizabeth Arden, *p. 141*
New York, NY.
Personal care products

El Torito Restaurants, *p. 94–95*
Irvine, CA.
Food service

Empire of America Federal Savings Bank, *pp. 23, 113*
Buffalo, NY.
Financial services

EPIC Healthcare, *p. 203*
Dallas, TX.
Hospital management

Episcopal Retirement Homes, *p. 115–16*
Cincinnati, OH.
Senior care services

Executive Life Insurance Company, *p. 120–21*
Los Angeles, CA.
Insurance services

Exxon Corporation, *p. 215*
New York, NY.
Petroleum products, exploration and refining, coal mining, chemical products

Federal Express, *pp. 6, 36, 40–41, 90, 92, 194, 202, 215*
Memphis, TN.
Delivery services

Fel-Pro, *p. 109*
Skokie, IL.
Gasket manufacturer

First Chicago, *pp. 31, 77, 148*
Chicago, IL.
Bank holding company

First-Knox National Bank, *p. 102*
Mount Vernon, OH.
Financial services

First of America Bank, *p. 39*
Libertyville, IL.
Banking company

First Pennsylvania Bank, *p. 82*
Philadelphia, PA.
Financial services

First Security Corporation, *p. 173*
Salt Lake City, UT.
Financial services

First Union Banks, *p. 118*
Charlotte, NC.
Financial services

Five Star Speakers, Trainers & Consultants, *p. 142*
Overland Park, KS.
Training and seminar services

Florida Power and Light, *p. 15*
North Palm Beach, FL.
Electric utility

Florists Transworld Delivery Assoc., *p. 60–61*
Southfield, MI.
Flower distributors and retailers

GTE Corporation,
pp. 124–26, 176
Stamford, CT.
Telecommunications,
electrical products,
laboratories

**Gunneson Group
International,** p. 52
Landing, NJ.
Total quality consulting
firm

Hallmark Cards,
pp. 202, 209, 212
Kansas City, MO.
Manufactures and sells
greeting cards, party
goods

Hardee's, p. 174–75
Rocky Mount, NC.
Fast food restaurants

**The Hartford Steam
Boiler Inspection and
Insurance Company,**
p. 60
Hartford, CT.
Boiler and machinery
insurance

Hatfield Quality Meats,
p. 221–22
Hatfield, PA.
Food processing

HealthTrust, p. 203
Nashville, TN.
Hospital management

Hecht's, p. 113
Arlington, VA.
Hardware stores

H. J. Heinz Company,
p. 38
Pittsburgh, PA.
Food processing
company

Herman Miller,
pp. 204, 216
Zeeland, MI.
Manufactures office
furniture

Hewitt Associates,
pp. 109, 126, 177, 220
Lincolnshire, IL.
Benefits and compen-
sation consulting

Hewlett-Packard,
pp. 9, 21, 73, 78, 130,
188, 212
Palo Alto, CA.
Manufacturer of
electronic measurement
and testing equipment
and computer products

**Hilton Hotels
Corporation,** p. 42
Beverly Hills, CA.
Hotels and casinos

Home Depot, pp. 36, 89
Atlanta, GA.
Home improvement
supply center

Honda of America,
pp. 111, 120
Marysville, OH.
Manufactures auto-
mobiles

Honeywell, p. 84–86
Minneapolis, MN.
Produces industrial
controls systems,
avionics equipment,
environmental controls
for home and buildings,
and navigational
equipment

**Hotel Association of New
York City,**
p. 176–77
New York, NY.
Hospitality

**Houghton Mifflin
Company,** p. 69–70
Boston, MA.
Publishing company

Hughes Missile, p. 149
Los Angeles, CA.
Weapons manufacturer

**Hyatt Hotel
Corporation,**
pp. 26–27, 38–39, 116,
219
Chicago, IL.
Hotels and industrial
companies

IBM, pp. 47, 48, 81,
110–11, 134, 188, 198,
216, 218
(International Business
Machines),
Armonk, NY.
Computer and business
machine manufacturer

**ICI Pharmaceuticals
Group,** p. 89

Wilmington, DE.
Pharmaceuticals

Indianapolis Power and Light Company, p. 23
Indianapolis, IN.
Electric utility

Inland Steel Industries, p. 37
Chicago, IL.
Steel producer and services

Integrated Genetics (see Gene-Trak Systems)

Intel Corporation, pp. 46, 91
Santa Clara, CA.
Manufacturers semi-conductors, memories, computer systems, software

Inter-Continental Hilton Head, p. 122
Hilton Head, SC.
Hotel

Internal Revenue Services, p. 51
(IRS), Ogden, UT.
Government agency

Interstate Electronics, p. 217
Anaheim, CA.
Electronic manufacturer

ITT, p. 102
New York, NY.
Insurance, defense, hotels, communication,

automotive fluid technology, forest products, finance, electronics

JASCO Tools, p. 149
Rochester, NY.
Tool manufacturing and sales

Jefferson County Community Center, p. 106
Lakewood, CO.
Community services

John Deere Dubuque Tractor Works, p. 106
Dubuque, IA.
Farm equipment

Johnson & Johnson, p. 218
New Brunswick, NJ.
Consumer products and pharmaceuticals

S. C. Johnson & Son, pp. 36, 37, 188, 210–11, 219
(Johnson Wax),
Racine, WI.
Manufacturer of house-hold and personal care products

Johnsonville Foods, pp. 147–48, 192
Sheboygan, WI.
Sausage manufacturer

Kellogg Company, p. 209
Battle Creek, MI.
Produces ready-to-eat cereals

King Copper Motel, p. 65
Copper Harbor, MI.
Motel

Knight-Ridder, p. 37
Miami, FL
International newspaper publishing and information services

Kollmorgen Corporation, p. 189
Stamford, CT.
Manufactures electro-optical instruments, electric motors, circuit boards

KXKT-FM, p. 141
Omaha, NE.
Radio station

Lavelle Aircraft Company, pp. 165–66, 218
Philadelphia, PA.
Transportation equipment

Leadership Synergy, p. 183
Scottsbluff, NE.
Medical billing company

LensCrafters, pp. 113, 128–29
Cincinnati, OH.
Optical stores

Leo Burnett Company, pp. 78, 130, 205, 212, 216, 220
Chicago, IL
Advertising agency

High-tech industrial products

RazorSoft International,
p. 133
Oklahoma City, OK.
Developer and
distributor of video
games

Reader's Digest, pp. 44,
196, 213, 217, 220, 225
Pleasantville, NY.
Publishing company

Recreational Equipment,
pp. 83, 220
(REI),
Seattle, WA.
Camping and hiking
equipment

Remington Products,
pp. 51–52, 174, 222
Bridgeport, CT.
Personal care products

**Republic Engineered
Steels,** p. 199
Massillon, OH.
Steel processing

**Resort Condominiums
International,** p. 137
Indianapolis, IN.
Telemarketing of time-
share condominiums

Rexair, p. 135
Troy, MI.
Sells cleaning systems

**Ridgeway Development
Corporation,** p. 103
Atlanta, GA.

Commercial and
residential real estate

ROLM Corporation,
pp. 45, 46, 213, 218
Santa Clara, CA.
Manufactures comput-
erized telephone
exchanges (PBX)

Rosenbluth Travel,
p. 35
Philadelphia, PA.
Travel agency

Ross Laboratories,
p. 162–65
Columbus, OH.
Manufactures pediatric,
pharmaceutical and
nutritional products

Royal Appliance, p. 65
Cleveland, OH.
Appliance manufacturer

Ryder, pp. 145, 210
Miami, FL.
Rents and leases trucks

Saga Corporation,
p. 213
Menlo Park, CA.
Food service

**Sample Service
Corporation,** p. 171
Long Island City, NY.
Swatch book distributor

San Diego, CA,
p. 11–13
Department of Social
Services, Local
government agency

**San Diego Convention
and Visitors Bureau,**
p. 123
San Diego, CA.
Tourism

**Saskatchewan
Telecommunications,**
p. 225
Regina, Saskatchewan,
Canada.
Telecommunications

**G. S. Schwartz and
Company,** p. 52
New York, NY.
Public relations firm

Science Applications,
p. 203
Falls Church, VA.
Research and
development

**Security Pacific
Corporation,** pp. 34, 216,
217–18
Los Angeles, CA.
Financial services

Servico Pacific, p. 66
Honolulu, HI.
Diversified sales
company

**Shearson Lehman
Brothers,** p. 179–80
Stamford, CT.
Insurance and financial
services

Shell Oil Company,
p. 196
Houston, TX.
Oil company

Taylor Corporation,
p. 54
North Mankato, MN.
Printing company

Tektronix, pp. 3–4, 40
Beaverton, OR.
Manufacturer of
oscilloscopes and other
electronic instruments

Tel Excell, p. 166
Seattle, WA.
Communication skills
consultants and speakers

Temps & Company,
p. 51
Washington, DC.
Temporary employment
agency

The Tennant Company,
p. 22
Minneapolis, MN.
Manufacturing company

Tenneco, pp. 189, 218
Houston, TX.
Pipeline operations,
manufacturer of farm and
construction equipment

**Tennessee Valley
Authority,** p. 151
Norris, TN.
Land resources

**Thomas J. Lipton
Company,** p. 98
Englewood Cliffs, NJ.
Food distributor and
manufacturer

**Thomson Consumer
Electronics,** p. 99
Circleville, OH.
Glass manufacturer

Time Warner, pp. 46,
78, 194, 217, 220
New York, NY.
Publishing company

Todays Temporary,
pp. 113, 153
Dallas, TX.
Temporary employment
agency

**Topps Manufacturing
Company,** p. 186
Mount Vernon, NY.
Makes baseball cards

**Total Training
Technology,** p. 34
Fairfax, VA.
Training consultants

Toyota, p. 63
Georgetown, KY.
Automobile
manufacturer

**The Travelers
Corporation,** p. 187
Hartford, CT.
Insurance company

Traveltrust Corporation,
p. 128
San Diego, CA.
Travel agency

Tri Companies, p. 33
Boston, MA.
Travel company

Tupperware, pp. 36, 178
Kissimee, FL.
Manufactures and
distributes food storage
containers

**United Insurance
Company of America,**
p. 136–37
Chicago, IL.
Insurance services

**United Postal Savings
Associates,** p. 138
St. Louis, MO.
Savings institution

**United Savings Bank
(FSB),** p. 135–36
San Francisco, CA.
Financial services

**United Services
Automobile Association,**
pp. 26, 140
San Antonio, TX.
Automobile and home
insurance company

Unitog Company,
p. 91
Kansas City, MO.
Maker of industrial uni-
forms and business
clothing

Valvoline Oil Company,
p. 187
Lexington, KY.
Refines and manufactures
auto lubricants,
chemicals and filters

**Veterans Administration
of Philadelphia,** pp. 48,

ABOUT BOB NELSON

BOB NELSON is founder of Nelson Motivation, Inc., and a vice president of Blanchard Training and Development, Inc., a leading training and consulting company located in San Diego, California. He has authored numerous books on management and business skills, including *Empowering Employees Through Delegation, Decision Point* and *We've Got to Start Meeting Like This: A Guide to Successful Business Meeting Management*. He holds an MBA from the University of California at Berkeley and is a doctoral candidate at The Peter F. Drucker Graduate Management Center of The Claremont Graduate School in suburban Los Angeles. He lives in San Diego.

Mr. Nelson writes a monthly column, "Rewarding Employees," available for company or association publications or internal training or distribution. For more information, contact:

Rewarding Employees
P.O. Box 500872
San Diego, CA 92150-9973
619-743-5030
619-673-9031 (fax)

Mr. Nelson is also available to speak at your company, association or conference or to consult with your organization on the topic of recognition, rewards and reward systems. For more information, contact:

1-800-575-5521
Nelson Motivation, Inc.
P.O. Box 500872
San Diego, CA 92150-9973
619-673-0690
619-673-9031 (fax)
E-mail: BobRewards@aol.com
Website: www.nelson-motivation.com

COMMENTS/CORRECTIONS/ADDITIONS

This book is updated each printing. If you have any comments, corrections or additions—including any resources that you'd like referenced in the Appendixes—please send them to the address below:

Rewarding Employees
P. O. Box 500872
San Diego, CA 92150-9973

If you have received or know of an exceptional employee reward or have a suggestion or recognition story that you'd like included in a subsequent edition of this book, please forward it with contact information to the above address.

NOTES

NOTES

NOTES

NOTES

NOTES

NOTES

NOTES

NOTES

NOTES